Alpha Male Bible
2 Books in 1

Become a Real Alpha Man; Develop
Confidence, Self-Discipline and Charisma
Through Psychology of Attraction, Small Talk
and Body Language

Thomas J. Young

Copyright © 2021 by Thomas J. Young

All rights reserved.

No part of this book may be reproduced in any form on by any electronic or mechanical means, including information storage and retrieval systems, without permission in writing from the publisher, except by a reviewer who may quote brief passages in a review.

Designed by : Nicholas Coren

Cover: Raphael Alphonso.

Printed in the United States of America

ARM Publishing LLC

May, 2021

Your Free Gift

As a way of saying thanks for your purchase, I wanted to offer you a free bonus E-book which is called **The Confidence Workbook** to the readers of this book!

To get access just click here- **Free Gift Download**

Join our FACEBOOK Group to learn and ask questions improving your communication skills.

Mind Mastery - The Art of Personal Development

Join Now

TABLE OF CONTENTS

Book - 1

Introduction	8
Chapter 1: Make a Killer First Impression	20
Chapter 2. Make Yourself Interesting	26
Chapter 3. Keep the conversation alive	32
Chapter 4. Master Non-Verbal Communication	40
Chapter 5. Know How to Make Eye Contact	46
Chapter 6. Make Others Feel Special - With Your Genuine Smile	50
Chapter 7. Develop Social Skills	54
Chapter 8. Build Self Confidence	68
Chapter 9. The Touch of Genuine Compliment	82
Chapter 10. Have Magnetic Personality	88
Chapter 11. Develop Meaningful Relationships	96
Conclusion	102
References	106

Book - 2

Introduction	112
Chapter 1. The Basics of Small Talk	116
Chapter 2. Mastering the Art of Small Talk	136
Chapter 3. Small Talk Topics	142
Chapter 4. Make Successful Small Talk	152
Chapter 5. How To Make Effortless Small Talk	162
Chapter 6. Overcoming Shyness And Fear	172
Chapter 7. Using Body Language in Small Talk	182
Chapter 8. Non-Verbal Communication and the Social Code	196
Chapter 9. Be a Good Storyteller	206
Chapter 10. Making Genuine Connections with People	212
Chapter 11. Ending Small Talks Gracefully	220
Chapter 12. Developing Your Conversations Skills	228
Chapter13. Forming and Growing Friendships	262
Chapter 14. Conversation	284
Conclusion	294

Book - 1

How To Talk To Anyone

51 Easy Conversation Starter and Tricks to Generate Deep Conversation, Make Real Friends, and Achieve Big Success in Relationships

Introduction

When you first picked this book up, you probably read the title and created this image in your head of what it would actually be like to have the ability to speak with anyone. Maybe you have a fantasy of telling stories around the water cooler, everyone wide-eyed at how good your stories are.

Maybe it's the same with your dating life, and you crave to be the charismatic boy or girl that charms all who listen to you. Perhaps you want to communicate better with your colleagues, managers, bosses, or clients.

Yikes! I'm sure you're starting to see how vastly communicating with others literally affects every part of your life! However, I want you to put these fantasies aside for now (I promise we'll make them become a reality later) because we need to start with you.

Yup. It's time to take a long, hard look at ourselves in the mirror because guess what? There's a reason why people say, "You can't love other people properly until you learn to love yourself first." It sounds philosophical and perhaps something you've heard before, but hear me out.

Anyone who communicates with others, whether by personal or business meetings, would benefit from learning how to establish relationships to improve communication. The general definition of relationship defines the connection between two or more people in sync or on the same wavelength. Think of a time when you felt absolutely in contact with someone you were with. This is a beautiful experience. You're relaxed and comfortable. You have a sense of confidence and are able to share personal knowledge on aspects of your life that could be avoided otherwise.

The word connection comes from an old French verb, the reporter, which literally means something back. Via the communication process, one person sends a message, and the other sends a message back. In the field of neurological programming (NLP), the relationship includes increasing the similarities between yourself and the person you are interacting with to build an environment of confidence, comfort, and emotional support.

We're going to make this actionable.

Let's start with the foundations of who you are, right here, right now. Your sense of self has to be defined because it will literally dictate how you act in every single situation from here on out, and you can either unconsciously let this happen, or you can be aware and in control of it. Don't worry; this will all make sense as we move forward.

A question to get the juices flowing:

Who are you?

Just consider and be aware of whatever thoughts come to mind. Now take those thoughts and drop the basic identity stuff, like your name, age, or your job. Now how do you see yourself? What kind of person do you associate yourself with? What beliefs and values do you have? Yup, we're jumping straight into the deep end here.

Your sense of self is everything. It defines you.

In the study of psychology, the sense of self is an all-encompassing view you have on yourself, your beliefs, your purpose in this world, and who you are. Guess what? If you don't know your sense of self, how can you expect to be yourself when you're around others?

Having a sense of self motivates you to get up in the morning because you're fully aware of your mission in life and what causes you're fighting for. You know where you stand and what matters to you. Now, that's not to say your sense of self can't and won't change over time. In fact, if it didn't change, this can also be unhealthy, commonly known as being stuck in your ways. However, having some idea of your sense of self is vital. You cannot be confident without it.

Erika Myers, a professional counselor, based in Oregon, sums it up perfectly.

"Having a well-developed sense of self is hugely beneficial in helping us make choices in life. From something as small as favorite foods to larger concerns like personal values, knowing what comes from our own self versus what comes from others allows us to live authentically."

Authentic living. Isn't that the dream? No, it's not a dream. It's a necessity.

When you can learn to be yourself authentically, you can then authentically be yourself with other people. Do you know how people say you can only really love others when you learn to love yourself? Well, we're playing on the same board as that ideology.

Being authentic means you know you're not perfect (and that nobody is). Still, you're willing to accept your flaws and simultaneously embrace your strengths because they define you more than anything.

A lack of a sense of self is a problem.

Without any ideas of who you are or what you stand for, you'll find yourself drifting through life. You'll be uncertain and indecisive. Your life will lack momentum and drive. You'll feel anxious and unsatisfied, but you won't be able to put your finger on why because you don't understand what you want and don't want.

Remember my friend Kyle at his sister's wedding? In many ways, his whole sense of self had been derived from his marriage, and he didn't know who he was without it. When speaking with others at the wedding, he was drifting.

Was he there to have a good time? To simply show his face and support his sister? Was he there to meet new people? Was he looking to date someone new or even to hook up with someone? None of these things are good or bad because it depends on the individual and their wants or needs. However, without understanding what these wants or needs are, nothing can be done about them, and so the perpetual loop of anxiety continues.

To stress once again, you can't have relationships with others until you learn to have a relationship with yourself, which brings us nicely to your first exercise in this book. Don't worry. While it may sound a bit overwhelming, we're going to break it down and do this together. I got you.

This book will guide you to have a conversation with anyone. That is why it is essential to understand a conversation first before proceeding to the following chapters in this book.

What is a conversation?

A conversation is referred to as a communication between two or more people, and that is interactive. Basically, a conversation involves two or more people who are talking together. It is a kind of speech happening symmetrically and informally and aims to establish and maintain social ties. Conversations require listening and giving feedback.

Conversations are seen as social interactions; therefore, they follow some etiquette rules and depend on the social situation. Rules focusing on communications are based on the cooperative principle. Lack of adherence to the standards leads to deterioration of a conversation, and in some cases, it comes to an end. The cooperative principle in conversations is categorized into four conversation maxims. The four categories are used to describe rational principles followed by individuals who adhere to the cooperative policy to enhance effective communication.

Maxim of Quality - It is comprised of supermaxim and submaxims. Supermaxim calls for individuals to make their contribution in a conversation authentic. Submaxims also call for people to avoid communicating what they believe is false and avoid saying things they do not have adequate evidence. The maxim of quality ensures that people make many informative contributions to suit the present reason for communication. Additionally, people should avoid making contributions that are informative beyond what is required.

Maxim of Relation/ Relevance - One should maintain relevance during a conversation. One should make contributions that are relevant to communication and only change where need be.

Maxim of Manner - The supermaxim calls for one to be perspicuous, whereas the submaxims, on the other hand, require one to avoid ambiguity, the vagueness of expression. One should try to be as brief and orderly as possible.

The above maxims provide vital guidelines that enhance successful communication. The contributions one makes in a conversation should entirely depend on what one had previously been saying.

Types of Conversations

When talking to another person, it is essential to understand the kind of conversation you two are in. You can easily understand this by checking on the direction of the communication you are having taken as well as its tone. Basing on direction and tone, conversations can be grouped into four major types. These are debate, dialogue, discourse, and diatribe.

Debate - A debate is defined as a competitive and two-way conversation. The main goal in such a conversation is winning an argument or convincing other people. An example is two university students who are from different political sides arguing over politics.

Dialogue - A dialogue is a two-way conversation that is cooperative. The main objective of a dialogue is exchanging information and building healthy relationships between two or more people. An example of dialogue is between two undecided university students communicating with each other in a bid to come up with the best student leaders to vote for.

Discourse - This is one-way and cooperative communication. The main aim of such a conversation is delivering information from a writer or speaker to readers or listeners. An example of a discourse conversation is a professor giving a lecture on public administration to students.

Diatribe - This is a one-way communication that is competitive. The aim of the conversation is to express emotions or browbeating people who disagree with you or to inspiring people who share similar perspectives with you. An example is a student talking about the outcomes of student leaders' elections.

Understanding the four types of conversation helps you to understand the form of communication you are engaging in, thus determining the function of the conversation. Identifying the purpose of a conversation helps you to speak things that are the center of the conversation. Misidentification leads to conversational pitfalls, where it loses focus and eventually ends.

Now, imagine yourself at a party. Drinks are flowing, music is playing, and everyone is having a great time. Where are you? Are you in the middle of the room, chatting and laughing, getting phone numbers, and making friends? Or are you in a corner, playing with your phone and wondering how to infiltrate this strange world filled with dynamic, interesting people? Now, imagine you are at a job interview. Your qualifications are stellar, your experience exhaustive, your references have nothing but praise for you. But, after the interview, you never receive a callback. What went wrong? Was it your choice of outfit? Did you answer the questions incorrectly?

Whether navigating the social world, the business world or just making friends out of people you meet, well-developed social skills are an absolute must. Shyness and social awkwardness are common ailments and nothing to be ashamed of, but they are liabilities. You might be funny and charming, intelligent and thoughtful, hardworking and trustworthy--but without the social skills to communicate well with others, how will anyone ever know the real you?

Why are social skills important, desired, and sought after?

The short answer is because people are wired to be social. We are naturally curious about other people and have a desire to connect with them. Our values, core beliefs, and identities are formed from our connection with other people and with groups with identities of their own. It's almost as if our solitary self is handicapped, and we need others to move us closer to wholeness, which enables us to make sense of ourselves and the world around us. However, to form these desired connections, we need social skills. But what exactly are social skills? A chapter of this book will define and describe these skills and discuss the challenges that make it challenging to overcome social fears. These chapters will also provide guidelines that will help you identify areas where you struggle with social interactions and questions and prompts that will help you set goals for success as you move forward with your social skills journey.

Your relationships with others, your job, yourself, and your levels of overall happiness and life satisfaction are all determined by your ability to communicate and connect. You could have millions of dollars in the bank, have everything that someone can be deemed successful for having, but if you're lonely, you're not happy.

You can be poor and materially have nothing, but if you're surrounded by caring people with whom you share a meaningful connection, and you can feel like the wealthiest person on the planet.

Being confident, charismatic, and open to connecting with others is not a trait you're born with. I used to believe that the confident people, those who could hold an entire audience or keep you hooked intimately on their every word, were gifted with a natural talent for confidence. I was wrong.

Confidence and charisma are skills that can be learned, honed, and practiced. They can even be mastered.

Have you ever gone into a room and saw that one person who dominates the conversation, maybe in a group of friends or in a meeting at work? Perhaps you had a friend who can seemingly speak to anyone about anything, and no matter the situation, they carry the flow of the conversation seemingly without effort? Ever found yourself envious of that person?

That's not the first time that person is doing that. You see years of practice. Years of trial and error. Years of making mistakes, practicing new techniques, and learning from each experience along the way. They would have had awkward moments in school, embarrassing meetings, and conversations, where nothing seemed to work.

And this all raises more questions.

How can you do things differently? How do you become confident? How can you talk to anyone about anything?

Final questions.

How do you get better at swimming? You spend time in the pool.

How do you get better at writing? You write.

How do you get better at connecting with people? You connect with people.

Like all life skills, confidence is an act that's practiced and honed over time, but like an athlete needs a coach, I'm writing this book to help guide you along the path of your own journey. First, we're going to cover your mindset and get that in check, so you're actually ready for meeting new people.

Then we're going on to the real meat of this book. This is where I will cover subjects like how to start a conversation with someone, find similar interests, and guide the conversation with questions. You'll also find out how to be more charismatic and confident and how to act and present yourself in any situation you may find yourself in.

This book aims to be the key that will unlock so many doors in your life through connection and opportunities. You will learn the best and most effective ways to not only handle all situations with confidence but to tap into your inner charm and charisma and dazzle and impress everyone with your conversation and social skills.

So, let's hang around no longer.

Chapter 1: Make a Killer First Impression

We all want to be remembered. But while it's nice to leave an excellent first impression, it takes some effort on your part. According to an article in Time Magazine (2006), it takes less than 1/10th of a second for our brains to process information about the patterns in a person's face when we meet them for the first time. Furthermore, this information converts into our first impressions about the qualities of those persons, including honesty, friendliness, morality, and trustworthiness (Willis & Todorov, 2006). This first impression tendency dates back prehistorically as a survival mechanism for early humans to gauge a stranger's intent to harm or help. Once we have interpreted our information, we use it to filter our communications. For instance, if you get a trustworthy first impression, you may be more likely to divulge personal information. If your first impression is negative, you may be more inclined to complain about the person to a friend or co-worker or avoid getting to know them at all.

You should consider first your context or venue. Where you are going that you want to make an excellent first impression is essential to how you may dress, how you posture yourself, behave, and what is expected. If your day is going badly, you may seem unapproachable. On the other hand, on a happy day, you may give off a better first impression. A frown or a sad look can appear problematic to someone you are meeting for the first time. They may see it as threatening or unfriendly. So, gauge whether your attitude is not good or bad, but practical or useless! It is certainly useless to act bored or rude. However, it is very useful to be enthusiastic. The good news is that you can train your attitude by creating one that is useful. All you have to do is make an eye contact while you are communicating - hopefully with a smile. Then you will have projected an open, warm, and positive first impression. Remember to refrain from crossing your arms, thereby appearing shut down or close-minded. If you are struggling to adjust your attitude, think back to a beautiful memory or make a quick gratitude list in your mind. Tell yourself something humorous before you walk into the room. Each day perform your daily attitude adjustment.

Those who find it easy to have an immediate connection with other people usually find some common ground within the first couple seconds of the conversation. Does this person have a similar article of clothing on? Do they have the new iPhone? Maybe they don't like wearing a tie or high heels. Also, note that if you are on the receiving end of a question ... people usually ask questions they want to answer themselves. For instance, "What did you do over the three-day weekend?" Naturally, you should answer the question and end it with an, "And you?"

With the right confidence, words, and body language, you can champion a captivating presence. People rarely remember a person who just stands there and doesn't say anything. You are much more likely to be noticed if you are participating actively in the conversation. Sharing stories, providing feedback, asking questions, and showing interest are some of the ways to make a lasting and positive first impression. People often don't want to say anything controversial, especially if you just met the person. But, without saying anything offensive, of course, you can still make a memorable statement. Sometimes being memorable is not the same as playing it safe. Speaking clearly about your mind with confidence makes you exciting and unique (aka memorable). Also, using the person's name with whom you are in conversation is a very effective means of being memorable. It tells that person they are important and that you care. A person's name is inherently linked to them. When individuals hear someone using their name, they immediately feel they are memorable because they remembered their name. That is, of course, if you say their name using the right tone. Remember to notice your tone as not to sound condescending or that you may be reprimanding them in some way.

To help you, use these tricks to make a positive first impression.

1: How To Be Upbeat And Smile.

A smile can make you happy and relaxed and can be infectious (more often). Greet the other person with a smile and let them know you can listen and have the answers to their problems. If you are smiling you can be regarded as a trustworthy person, as long as it remains genuine.

2: How To Remember The Person's Name And Use It Frequently.

Remembering and using the person's name will give a feeling of being essential or recognized. Try to save their names in your short-term memory, at least immediately. You will, of course, impress the people you meet, and you will be able to keep notes and suggestions linked with the right people. This is very helpful when you encounter more people than you expected.

3: How To Dress To Impress

Whether you are in a social, casual, or business atmosphere, your appearance is a huge part of an initial impression. You don't have to walk out and buy a Roberto Cavalli or Armani suit dress to impress someone (especially if you are a fellow!).

How you look signifies the way you take care of yourself and reflects self-respect. I am not talking about just dressing appropriately. Your behavior has to match. The rule of action speaking louder than words goes the same for your personal appearance. If you are able o dress casually for work, remember that there is such a thing as too casual.

4: How To Try Your Best Not To Be Overly Talkative

There is always the 70/30 rule as a guideline: you talk 30% and let the other person talk 70%. It can be very exciting meeting someone new, but try your best not to discuss too much of your personal interests, especially if it is a work gathering. Once you get to know someone, you can then share your personal context.

5: How To Listen And Never Look Uninterested

It doesn't matter if you are at a party, a networking event, or interviewing for a job. There are a lot of things happening when you are out and meeting new people. Shaking people's hands, asking their names, remembering their names, and for those suffering from social anxiety, there is a good chance of having to start a conversation. Everyone makes missteps and mistakes that don't really reflect who they are, but one of the biggest mistakes is seeming disinterested. So let them talk and just be a good listener with brief remarks like 'I understand' or 'I agree.' They want to be understood.

6: How To Be Organized

Practice, practice, practice! Whether you have to give a presentation, formal or informal, or just chat about a few new ideas, keep all your ducks in a row. Have your records in order and ensure that you have ample copies before you arrive. Know in what order you want your points to be discussed. Let them see that you planned ahead and know how to arrange your thoughts.

7: How To Be Respectful

Be polite. In fact, this is one of the essential ways to make a good impression, but it is often repeated. There is nothing as good as good manners and kindness that impresses.

As you can see from these ways to enhance your first impression, they are all linked to your behavior. What you do is show people how they can look forward to your future behavior. It can make a difference not only in remembering you but also in thinking about you!

Chapter 2. Make Yourself Interesting

If you want people to reach for you themselves, you need to become an interesting conversationalist. How can you find out how interesting you are to others? Do you know yourself? Many people still do not know themselves. There is no time to think about yourself in your daily routine.

Take the time to write out everything that you know about yourself, your advantages and disadvantages, what pleases you, and what annoys you. You will learn a lot about yourself. Accept yourself and love. These tips sound very simple, but they are not so simple to implement because all our problems begin in childhood.

To accept yourself, use a simple technique.

Remember the times from childhood when your parents criticized you and were unhappy with you. Remember, in detail. Now think about it. Our parents are ordinary people who made usual mistakes, no worse than everyone else. Your mother dreamed that her child was the best. She needed this to feel successful, a good mother. It was a long time ago. You have grown up. You are already adults, independent people. Today you have the right to perceive your childhood achievements and failures differently.

Write about what you did well in your life. What did you achieve? What is your merit? How were you honored? Write about all the good. At first glance, minor achievements, combined, can make up a weighty volume of victories. You will be surprised to find that you have achieved a lot.

If you never kept a diary, it's time to start. Let it be a diary of your achievements.

Every night before going to bed, write down what successes and victories you had during the day.

You do not have to be able to know everything and always know the correct answer, just as you do not have to like everyone. Moreover, this is impossible! Allow yourself to be mistaken!

Here are some tricks you can use to make yourself interesting to others:

8: How To Forgive Yourself For Mistakes.

It is just the mistakes and their analysis that lead us ultimately to success.

9: How To Analyze Your Attitude To Criticism.

Perhaps you are too obsessed with it. Not many people know how to criticize correctly. Often, negative comments addressed to someone else are caused by envy or the critic's own problems. Remember the facts. Do not believe everything you hear.

Be proud of yourself. Celebrate your successes. Often we scold ourselves for failures, and what is done well, we take for granted. You have put your work and knowledge into the achieved result. Appreciate it. Thank the world that allowed you to create it. Enjoy the moment.

Emotions become a resource the moment we control them. Most often, we are driven by unconscious emotional habits. And it does not occur to us that the fault of the project, the failure of negotiations, or the loss of an important partner was our unconstructive emotional state.

Therefore, love yourself, accept and maintain your good emotional state.

10: How To Volunteer Your Time

Volunteering your time is a win-win for everyone involved.

Not only are you dedicating some time of your life to help others and actually benefit the communities or causes you're working for, but you also become more interesting because of the experiences you're getting involved in.

11: How To Embrace Fear

An actionable tip you can try right now. Whenever you go to do something new, or you're entering an experience that you aren't sure about, do you get that little pang in your stomach? That fear that you don't really know how to move forward? Notice that feeling and try to step through it. Embrace the fear, and don't let it hold you back.

Will Smith famously said in an interview that "Everything that's good in life can be found on the other side of fear." You just need to take the leap of faith in yourself. Remember, the fear of being uninteresting makes you uninteresting. These emotions shut you down and hold you in place, rather than allowing you to live free.

12: How To Make Interesting Conversations

If you're asking someone how they are, but you don't really care about the answer, this is going to show up like a house on fire.

Lazy, uninteresting people stick to small-talk topics like the weather and ask if they're watching any good TV series (remember that watching most TV is just a passive activity that won't really bring you any gain), or ask what you do for a career. BORING! It's fine every now and then, and when you're starting out, but after everything you've read so far, you're definitely beyond this point now.

Instead of boring topics, open the doorway to new, interesting conversations, like asking what personal projects someone is working on, what the weirdest thing they have ever eaten is, what items you could find on their bucket list, or if they're learning any new skills.

Getting answers to these questions can introduce you to whole new worlds that you didn't even know existed. You never know—you might be introduced to something new that you love, or you may learn something new that changes your life.

13: How To Try New Hobbies

These are all the things you care about. Now figure out which hobbies you love the most and which ones you want to get involved in. Make time for them and enjoy the experience you have doing them! Not only will you meet new people, but you'll also have interesting things to talk about with others!

Chapter 3. Keep the Conversation Alive

Believe it or not, at one moment or another, most people feel uncomfortable or uninterested about other people. There are so many things that can make all of us like this. And that's exactly how conversation easily end up.

Conversations are seen as social constructs that help in building and maintaining relationships. It may involve a basic dialogue where people communicate their thoughts and ideas to other people. Conversations carry with them the opportunities to learn new ideas as well as present your own information.

When you need to speak with a professional or a stranger, you may not have enough time to consider the terms and patterns of a conversation. Unlike when you're excitedly talking to a friend or relative about a song you're about to release, a stranger may think you're trying to convince them to buy the song. Some people are aware that they are ineffective at conversing and participating in social situations, but they console themselves with the thought that there is some sort of link between a high IQ and an inability to hold a decent conversation.

According to TV shows like The Big Bang Theory, extremely intelligent people are often socially awkward, but this doesn't matter because they are extremely intelligent in other ways.

There are two problems with this line of thinking. The first is that there is no scientific evidence linking genius to poor social functioning. This theory is contradicted by numerous individual examples. Albert Einstein was charming and socially successful, despite being widely regarded as one of the most brilliant people ever to live. The second issue is that, even if there is a proven negative correlation between IQ and social skill, it is important to remember that the majority of us are not.

Even if intelligence were enough to guarantee success in life, we couldn't all get by on it. Given the frailty of the human ego, this is a difficult truth for some of us to accept. Fortunately, whether or not you have a brilliant mind, you can learn how to have effective social interactions with others.

To be able to keep the conversation alive, here are some tricks you can use:

14: How To Start Conversations with Questions

Of course, one of the most powerful ways to use questions is by using them to *initiate* conversations in the first place. However, you don't want to be boring. There's no denying the tried and tested questions like "How are you?" and "Where are you from?" are boring and too generic. These aren't the best ways to start a conversation. There are definitely better options to choose from.

So, let's break it down.

First, you need to get the conversation going. I'm going to assume you're not just talking to a random stranger on the street, but perhaps talking to a colleague at work, or a new client, as part of a networking event while on a date with someone, or so on.

As a side note, however, If you did want to talk to a stranger on the street, then always start with a conversation about something in the immediate environment, such as asking for directions, a good place to eat, the time, or commenting on something that is going on around you.

For example, if there's a carnival happening, you could ask something like, "When was the last time you went to one of these?"

For brevity, let's say you're talking to someone you know in a familiar place. It's time to get involved with some decent conversations. Here are some questions you could ask that can open a great conversation in various situations.

Tell me something about yourself?

This is a great question because you let the other person take control and tell them what they want you to know, because of course, no one is going to tell you something they don't want you to know, allowing you to have a real insight into who this person is and what they're all about.

What was your highlight of this week?

This is one of my favorite questions because it allows the

conversation to take a positive tone and allows the other person to really think about what matters to them. When they're thinking about positive things, they're going to be feeling positive emotions. It's far better than "How are you?"

Are you working at this moment that excites you?

Another chance for someone to get excited about talking to you, this question is ideal for when you want someone to be passionate with. Of course, they'll talk about the most important thing in their life, another great way to get to know someone and see what matters to them.

Have you been here before?

An open-ended question you can use to gauge someone's familiar with a place or person. If you're in a meeting or at an event, such as a business meeting, social event, birthday party (did you come last year?) and so on, you'll get a nice idea of how connected this person is.

15: How Not To Get Trapped In A Conversation Topic

Don't get trapped in a conversation topic when neither you nor the other person is interested. If you can tell that both of you find the conversation uninteresting, segue to a different topic.

16: How To Talk About The Day

This is one of the small talks you can use when you have no clear idea of which topic to start with and break the silence. Talking about the day may either be about your day or their day, depending on whichever you decide to choose from. Even those having bad days can build a conversation by making it brighter. However, ensure you avoid engaging in personal matters which may feel offensive or sometimes invasion of privacy. Make it enjoyable, mainly when the other person participates in the conversation freely.

17: How Not To Let Your Mouth Move Faster Than Your Mind

Instead of talking when you're not sure what to say, pause for a moment and collect your thoughts. Nobody will mind a short delay, and when you speak, you'll sound much more polished.

18: How To Find The Connection

Now you're talking with someone you've approached the right way, the ice has broken, and the conversation is starting to pick up and find its place. What do you do now?

The best approach for finding a connection is to find similarities you have with that other person. This means finding common ground on things you're interested in, whether that's a hobby, passion, or music taste, or even just commenting and sharing opinions of what is happening in the immediate environment or situation you're in. An example of the latter would be commenting on the music at a concert you're at.

This is where your listening skills come into play because you're focusing on what someone is saying (and what their body language is saying) and then picking out the bits they seem most connected to, then running with it. Let me give you an example.

Let's say you're at a concert and you're engaging in small talk with someone at the bar. Your first impression is that they are not really having a good time. They just look into their drink, not really focusing on the music, and seem to be mentally somewhere else.

Everything about them suggests they're having a rough time, so you choose to act compassionately and ask if everything's okay, perhaps saying something like, "Is the music too loud for you?" This is lighthearted, not too personal, but also suggesting that you know that something isn't right, and you're willing to talk to them about it.

Depending on their answer, you can then figure out what's wrong and how you can deal with the situation, and you could be on the road to making a close friend.

19: How To Reference Your Social Context

When you're starting a conversation with someone, reference

your social context for your first topic. For instance, if you see someone in class, start the conversation by asking them what they thought of the test you took yesterday. If you see someone at a party, ask them how they know the party's host.

Chapter 4. Master Non-Verbal Communication

Words are our main communication form. Words are able to make us happy or unhappy, worsened or elated. How can anything with no actual material truth mentally and physically have such a strong impact on us? There's really old thinking that gives you an idea about how we can get out of the consequences of other people's words: "If someone gives you a gift and you don't acknowledge it, who would that include it? If someone threw a pillow at you and you didn't respond to it, then it might bounce and fall off.

How the sense of words is perceived is based on one's own views, which are actually counterproductive to world perceptions. Your subjective views are the curtain between you and the universe. Every word, sound, scent, vision, and interaction reaching your mind and intellect is hidden by this subjective veil of perception.

Nevertheless, when having a conversation with anyone, it is also important to notice and acknowledge the non-verbal cues.

Imagine you are talking to a coworker in your company break room. While she is carrying on a conversation with you, she is also toying with her phone and not making eye contact. Would you imagine she is interested in your conversation or simply killing time until it's time to go back to work?

Any time you speak, about half of your message is carried through your words. The other half is carried through nonverbal cues: your tone of voice, facial expressions, posture, and gestures. No matter what you are saying, if your nonverbal cues don't match your message, you won't be believed. Take the example above; the distracted coworker might be fully engaged in her conversation with you, but her body language says she is bored and disinterested. Likewise, even if you know that you are giving someone your complete attention, if you look at your shoes, turn your body away from them, or fidget with your keys or phone, the other person has no reason to believe you are focused on them. No one wants to talk to someone who doesn't want to be engaged.

So, can you make your body language match your message? Can you control your facial expression and gestures? Can you make the person you are talking to feel like you are interested and focused on them? The answer is yes to all of the above--you can make your body language match your verbal language easily. But would it feel forced? Can others sense when you are trying too hard to make eye contact and smile? The answer is no--if you know how to use body language to your advantage.

Eye contact and smiling are only two pieces of the body language puzzle. There are myriad other ways people communicate ideas, emotions, and their state of mind nonverbally. Let's start with the face. Suppose you are talking to a neighbor, and she names a person or place you are not familiar with. Likely, your brows will furrow slightly, or your head may tilt a bit to the side. Your neighbor may see this and know that you didn't quite get what she said, giving her an opportunity to clarify her statement. If she doesn't, you may spend the rest of the conversation wondering about "Linda from Harlingen." Here, you can see how important reading nonverbal cues are. Were your roles reversed, you wouldn't want your neighbor wondering who and what you are talking about?

To master non-verbal communication, here are some tricks you can use:

20: How To Observe Body Language

Learning to read and interpret body language is a critical skill, yet not a difficult one to develop. Generally, if a person positions their body toward you and their arms are at their sides, they are open and receptive. Likewise, if they turn away from you, fold their arms across their chest, and cross their legs, they are "closed off"--creating a barrier between you and themselves to signify they are not open to talking.

Let's consider a more formal setting, such as the workplace. If you are meeting with a supervisor for a performance evaluation, you may give off defensive body language: keeping your hands and gestures close to your body, sitting cross-legged, minimizing facial expressions, avoiding eye contact. Your supervisor may wonder why you have the need to feel defensive--are you concerned about your own poor work performance? Are you hiding something from him? If your roles were reversed, how would you feel about someone else's defensive body language?

21: How To Be Relaxed

Relaxation implies that you are confident with whatever you are communicating. Therefore, be at ease when making the communication; sit or stand upright while your hands by your sides (do not pocket). Similarly, do not support your hands on the hips as that shows aggression or dominancy.

22: How To Use Firm Handshakes

Psychologists have established that much can be deduced from a handshake. Firstly, a loose handshake indicates awkwardness or lack of confidence. Therefore, when prompted to do so, use a firm handshake.

23: How Not To Scratch Your Head Or Touch Your Face

Scratching the head means you are cooking whatever you want to say. The main causes are that you are not well versed with the issue that needs to be addressed, the same case as touching your face. Perhaps you are subjected to respond to an issue that you are not sure of, state that you do not know. Otherwise, scratching your head and touching your face shows that whatever you want to say is not valid, or it is diluted.

Chapter 5. Know How to Make Eye Contact

Think of how many common sayings and idioms contain the word "eyes." Someone untrustworthy can be described as "shifty-eyed." A romantic interest might give you "bedroom eyes." You might describe someone you care for as the "apple of your eye." We are told to keep our "eyes on the prize" in competitions. Most everyone has heard the saying, "the eyes are the windows to the soul."

People make eye contact as a means to gain feedback. We often subconsciously check for eye contact when we ask a question and during conversation pauses. Eye contact is also used as a means of synchronization; we glance into each other's eyes' at grammatical stops and at the ends of statements to "pass the baton," so to speak, and invite the other to contribute. Eye contact represents interest, honesty, integrity--in short, making eye contact is vital to communicating with the world.

The psychology behind eye contact can be daunting, but with a little practice, making appropriate eye contact with another is as natural as looking through a window. In fact, in a sense, you are looking through a window--a window into another person's thoughts and feelings. Simply keep these tricks in mind:

24: How To Initiate Eye Contact.

Don't be afraid to look someone in the eye, even if they don't seem to respond. It may be that the person you are talking to is as wary of eye contact as you are. So, if you attempt to make eye contact and they don't reciprocate, don't take this as a sign that they are disinterested. Simply try again in a few moments.

25: How Not To Stare.

If you attempt eye contact twice, and the other person doesn't respond, give up. Again, this may simply be because they themselves have trouble with eye contact and should not be automatically taken to mean they don't want to talk to you. This is especially relevant when speaking with someone of another nationality, as different cultures have different rules regarding eye contact.

26: How To Know When To Look Away.

While eye contact is important, it is also important not to keep a laser-intense gaze on your subject. Too much eye contact can seem impersonal and, well, creepy. Look away every few seconds to another part of the person's face or elsewhere on their person, then re-initiate eye contact after a couple of seconds.

27: How To Use Other Forms Of Nonverbal Communication In Conjunction With Eye Contact.

Lean back when making eye contact with someone you don't yet know well. This will show that you respect their personal space; likewise, if they are talking about something personal or important to them, lean in slightly. This will show that you are focused on listening to them.

28: How Not To Focus Too Hard On Eye Contact.

Don't forget to look at a mutual topic of interest during a conversation or watch where you are going while walking. It is natural to look away from the person you are speaking to every few moments.

Seem like a lot to remember? Practice your eye contact skills with the following method: while talking to someone, look at one eye for three seconds, then the other eye for three seconds, then their mouth for three seconds. Every few moments, look away from their face for three seconds. Estimate the time, don't tick the seconds off in your head. This will help you develop the natural rhythm for eye contact.

It may also help you to raise your eyebrows slightly when making eye contact with someone. This helps you keep a neutral yet interesting facial expression. Some people feel their eyebrows drift down during conversations, giving the impression that they are frowning or glowering. If you catch yourself doing this, simply take a breath, raise your eyebrows or widen your eyes a bit (but not into a "shocked" expression), and resume your eye contact pattern.

Chapter 6. Make Others Feel Special - With Your Genuine Smile

While eye contact and other aspects of nonverbal communication can vary between cultures, a smile is universal. It signifies goodwill, friendliness, and acceptance across the globe. It is also automatic; you don't control your smile when you hear or see something pleasing. It simply happens. You can, of course, smile whenever you like. But, if not done correctly, a forced smile looks just that way--forced.

Think of a group photo where some people are smiling naturally, and others are forcing a smile. You can pick out the forced smiles every time--they look strained rather than happy and relaxed. Some people counteract this by making goofy faces, which is not advised, and some people simply don't smile if they feel they have to force it. Either way, you can tell who is having a good time and who is just going through the motions.

Your smile doesn't have to look forced. Have you ever been in a retail environment and noticed the cashier smiling at his customers? His smile looks natural and comes easily because he has practiced it over hundreds, if not thousands, of customer interactions. You don't need to talk to hundreds, thousands, or even dozens of people to gain the same natural, genuine smile

Smile and be Positive

Everyone has some sort of self-description. Maybe I'm an adventurous traveler and writer, maybe you're a sarcastic musician and comedian. However you define yourself, add "happy and positive" to the beginning of that description, and be that version of yourself.

People will decide how much time to spend with you primarily based on how they feel when they're around you. Your accomplishments are just enough to get people to want to know you. Whether or not they become good friends with you will have a lot more to do with how they feel while hanging out with you.

If you are cheerful and positive, people will enjoy spending time around you. The happy and positive version of you is the best version you have to offer other people. If someone is happy and in a great mood, your positivity will only make them feel even better. If someone is having a tough time, your positivity might cheer them up, or at least make them forget their problems for the time.

That doesn't mean you have to joke around all the time, be fake, or be rambunctious. You just want to be positive. Smile and look at the bright side. That's all it takes.

Positivity is even more important in groups than it is one-on-one. Seven happy excited people can have the wind taken out of their sails by one negative person acting alone. If seven people are having a good time and you end that, you're doing a lot of damage to people that you consider friends.

Just keep these tricks in mind.

29: How Not To Limit Your Smile To Your Mouth

When you smile naturally, your entire face lights up: your cheeks lift, your eyes sparkle, your nose crinkles slightly. If you just move your mouth into the position of a smile without the rest of your face following suit, your smile will be fake and unnatural. Practice this in a mirror: find something that you enjoy (a funny YouTube video or remembering a favorite joke) and let it make you smile. Notice how your entire face is invested in the smile. Then, clear your mind, and force a smile. See the difference?

You can smile with just your eyes.

Manipulating your eyes to look how they do when you're smiling can bring a smile to your face without moving your mouth. While smiling in a mirror, cover the lower half of your face and focus on your eyes. Then, while not smiling, practice manipulating your eyes to achieve the same effect.

30: How To Practice Makes Perfect Smile.

Exercise your smiling muscles in the mirror: smile and hold it for ten seconds, then widen your smile and hold for another ten seconds. Repeat this exercise daily. The muscles in your face can be strengthened and toned the same as any other muscles, making your smile come more naturally.

31: How To Learn When To Smile.

Obviously, no one smiles continuously. A natural smile lasts about as long as natural eye contact--about three to five seconds. Also, some people are nervous laughers; they smile and laugh intense or awkward situations as a way to mitigate some of their discomforts. This can be seen as inappropriate, though, so if you find yourself smiling when no one else is, give yourself a neutral expression. Try to smile when the person you are speaking with smiles, but don't match them smile for a smile--they will likely notice.

Chapter 7. Develop Social Skills

What makes human beings different from other lower animals is their ability to communicate through language and create friendships. Through communication, people interact with the aim of meeting different needs. What enables a human being to communicate and interact with others is social skills. This article aims at offering you helpful tips on how to improve your social skills, how to set goals, the importance of empathy, and how to meet people and make friends. The article will also offer helpful information on how to understand yourself and others as well.

Definition and Importance of Social Skills

Social skills are the competencies that help human beings to communicate, interact, and create peaceful interpersonal relationships. Social interaction has a variety of ingredients, including the ability to communicate, influence, and build harmonious relations. There are different levels of communication. These include interpersonal communication, group communication, social media communication, and communication through the mainstream media. Communication can also be grouped as underwritten, verbal, and nonverbal. While written communication entails communicating through written symbols, verbal communication is the process of sending a message through a spoken word. When you communicate orally, you're supposed to utilize various nonverbal cues of communication. These are cues, gestures, and facial expressions that you apply when talking.

Social skills are central when you're involved in any communication act. Having these skills enables you to interact with people excellently. Furthermore, when you possess social skills, people will pay attention to your message. There are various benefits of social skills. These include:

Creation of a friendly work environment

People who possess social skills are able to interact well with others and lessen incidents of conflicts. Leaders with social skills are able to understand others and apply persuasive techniques to influence them.

Knowledge acquisition

When you possess excellent social skills, you're able to interact with people from various backgrounds and gain much knowledge. The knowledge that you acquire assists you in lessening conflict.

Expansion of your network

When you possess social skills, you're likely to communicate with many people from diverse backgrounds. Some of these people may have opportunities that will assist you in improving your economic life.

Offering your perspectives

When you possess excellent social skills, you're able to provide your own perspectives on different matters. These perspectives may assist other people.

Focused

With social skills, you're able to get focused on attaining shared objectives.

Expansion of your business

When you possess admirable social skills, people will say something good about you, which may make others get attracted to your services. Through these referrals, you're likely to expand your business with a minimal amount spent on advertising.

Strengthen the relationships

You may not have enough social skills; you just have to walk in love. This affection is first expressed to those close to you, such as family and friends. I still look forward to those in your corner. Spend a nice time with them and enjoy your presence. And wherever possible, be there for them.

Qualities That Enhance Social Skills

Social skills are essential to anybody who wants to be successful in life. This is because these skills help us to create and nurture relationships. In case you want to improve on your social skills, there are a variety of qualities that you should adopt. These are as follows:

Effective Communication - Communication is an essential component of social skills. Communication will assist you in articulating your thoughts effectively and bringing them to the fore. When you're good at communication, you're able to put a team together with the intention of achieving goals.

Conflict resolution - In any social environment, conflicts sometimes emerge. In case you're a leader with excellent social skills, you're able to resolve these conflicts harmoniously.

Active listening - To listen actively means that you pay attention to whatever is said. When you pay attention to the other party, they will highly respect you. There are different strategies that you can employ to be an active listener. These include: avoiding distractions, concentrating on what is said, and getting well prepared to comment or ask questions.

Empathy - Empathy enables you to put yourself in other people's situations and identifying with their emotions. An empathetic person keenly evaluates the feelings of others. By developing empathetic skills, you're able to create strong relationships with other people.

Relationship Management - Social skills are essential in relationship management. When you manage a relationship, it means that you're able to connect with specific clients and develop strong bonds with them.

Respect - Respect is an essential component of communication. When you respect others, you're able to let them say things without interruption. You also appreciate people when communicating by asking thoughtful and relevant questions, being focused on the topic, and avoiding time wastage.

How to Be More Talkative

For the most part, barbecues, parties, lunches, and weddings produce pictures of food, interesting people, and a relaxing time. For some, these social events look like nightmares.

Are you now tired of watching social butterflies (or moths) flit from one party to another, exuding confidence and jolly laughter as you clutch your glass and grit your teeth nervously, waiting for the second hand to slowly tick by?

It's easy to ignore the value of informal functions but believe it or not, many remarkable events take place at these events - deals are closed, opportunities knock, and kindred spirits unite.

Make yourself a social butterfly by recalling these crucial points:

Be open

Take a profound pause. Smile. Smile. Relax. Relax. Look around to see if someone's like you and standing alone. You would be shocked to find out that other people are anxious. If they smile in return, approach them. Start with a 'Hello' and let the talk flow.

It's totally OK if nobody talks for a while - every now and then, we have to breathe (and eat or drink). Being a good listener is also a part of being a good conversationalist.

Don't be a wallflower - follow the lines at the buffet table and talk while filling your plate. Speaking of food is easy and draws the attention of people immediately. Remember to make your comments transparent and constructive. Keep your grievances to yourself!

A simple way to ensure you don't shy from the crowd is to chat with (and ideally get to know) at least three new people while you engage in a social event.

Be able

Since you want to socialize, you can start or direct a conversation with a few questions about everyday topics. Closed questions allow another person to quickly answer a "yes" or a "no and whether they want to explain further.

Open questions invite someone else to explore the subject in-depth and assist you both in seeking common areas of interest. If you have ideas about furnishings and decorations, food, and people around you will give you ideas of what to say and what to ask.

In each case, critical people skills for success include sample scripts with selected answers for common conversational scenarios for small interactions at work, meetings, social activities, on the phone, or in public places.

In addition to daily subjects, your personal favorites are also interesting topics to chat about. Are you familiar with news (local business, etc.) and pop culture (blogs, music, etc.)? Have you just returned from a holiday? Or did you just begin a hobby?

If you're lucky, you may find someone you can immediately click on, but be careful not to ignore others in the room.

Take a mental note for the exchange of touch and the interaction with your sons and daughters.

Be yourself.

"I am boring, however!"

The lamentation of my students is reminiscent of my mind, but a helpful "Involved is interesting."

No one is more fascinating than someone truly interested in hearing what you are saying. In the film, the leading character, Paul Tannek, seems the most socially awkward to reach New York, but recalls his father's advice and applies it to himself when he tries to make friends.

Off the silver screen, one day at Chili's, I was lunching alone when the waitress came to take my order. She asked me about my pregnancy after she did her work, and then the topic moved to obstetrics, television dramas such as Grey's Anatomy and House, and further studies.

Instead of lunching alone, I finally met a young, articulate, and smart man who was on the road to medical study, and I hope that he will be one of the most promising people in our country.

The point? The point? I wouldn't have given him a new look, as he was dressed in shirts and jeans as today's teenager, but when his questions were insightful and genuine, he got my attention.

Be sensitive

Although the young man above began a discussion successfully with a stranger about an unusual subject, personal remarks or questions that affect the age, appearance, ethnic background, marital status, political attachments, and financial background – i.e., salary or rent-a-house – are still very sensitive for most people.

Many also do not remember that informal functions, particularly those for the workplace, are for people to get to know each other better, but they are also a snake pit for scandals, as on Mondays, you can return to work.

So always keep in mind your Ps and Qs, stay away from joking (both the practice and the person), and stick to healthy conversation topics.

Finally, few would care to talk if you addressed the question "How do you do?" by divulging your health condition painfully or by sighing about family, money, or marital issues. In reality, the interested parties are usually the office gossip, Nosey Parkers, insurance, and multi-level marketing agents.

So, the following are tricks on how to improve your social skills:

32: How To Grow Self Awareness

Be a person who feels relaxed. Be aware of how you manage problems. Just because things don't go your way doesn't mean that everybody has to snap and be explosive. People enjoy the sight of calm people. Learn how to make the best of each situation regardless of how poor it might seem.

A flourishing personality

You cannot be rude, sullen, or brooding. If it is, you're preventing it now. This form of conduct stuns the development of an individual. Nobody wants to be around this kind of guy. True change starts from the inside. Start thinking about things that are perfect, pure, and just.

Make an assessment of yourself. Who better knows you than you? Create a list of all that you think needs to be changed and work on it. Work to make yourself stronger. We should all make some changes.

Do not be hypocritical. Be true to your strategy, your conversation, and your interest. Do not approach people for egotistical purposes. When you have hidden motives, people will see it.

33: How To Improve Empathy

Empathy is the ability to identify with other people's feelings. An empathetic person is able to understand another person's feelings and offer a solution. For example the story of good Samaritan, The Samaritan showed kindness and compassion to a Jew who was attacked and deprived of all by bandits. We should all walk in this kind of love that displays compassion and kindness to those in need. Keep the door open for someone with full hands, volunteer in your neighborhood, inspire a child. These kinds of actions will work miracles for you and the individual.

There are various components of empathy that you need to develop. These include:

Listening skills - An empathetic person has good listening skills. When you have excellent listening skills, it means that you don't interrupt others when they're talking. You ask relevant questions and make well-thought comments. It's essential to learn to be empathetic as people will confide in you.

Attentiveness - Being attentive means that you get more focused on listening to what the other person is saying. It would be best to avoid any distractions that will make you not listen attentively. You should also avoid interrupting the other party when they're talking.

Appreciate other people's cultures - You develop empathetic skills when you learn to respect other people's cultures. This requires that you travel a lot to meet new people from diverse cultural backgrounds. When you understand the reasons why people behave the way they do, you'll be empathetic and learn to appreciate them without any biases.

Request for feedback - It's advisable to request your close friends to offer you suggestions on how you should enhance your listening skills. After getting the feedback, come up with a strategy for implementing the recommendations. It would be best if you also learned to practice various aspects that you're enhancing.

Reading - There are different books that explore the topic of empathy. It's essential to look for these books and read them to improve your empathy skills. You can also look for valuable materials on the internet that shed light on the subject of empathy.

Evaluate your biases - To be able to be empathetic, it's essential to examine the biases that we have about others, which prevents us from listening to them empathetically. Maybe you're biased against somebody because of their race, color, or gender. When you remove these biases, you'll improve your empathetic skills.

Be curious - when you're curious, you need to listen to other people's stories regardless of their background. This curiosity will enable you to improve your empathy because you'll take time to listen to people you would never have heard in the first place.

Frame right questions - The kind of questions that you ask will determine the amount of empathy that you'll display. It's essential to learn to ask the right questions that are relevant to the subject under discussion.

34: How Not To Let Fear Hold You Back

All of us need to face our fears in life. Fear is an emotion that can make your belly get backflips, make you feel nauseous, and throw you off your game completely... If you really let it!

So many in this world take the easy route throughout their lives, allowing chances to slip by their fear.

There are all kinds of fears, but I will speak today about the fear of exposure. Now I'm not talking about being exposed literally (i.e., naked), but it's a legitimate concern for others, I'm sure! No, I'm talking about being profoundly exposed, taking your reputation away, and opening yourself up for inspection by others. It takes a lot of good luck; to face it, no one likes to be criticized, particularly when it comes to your reputation. What steps should you take to fight and work for you against the negative effect of this fear?

Foster Your Self-confidence

This fear of exposure increases to unmanaged levels without self-confidence, which eventually leads to failure. Surround yourself with constructive individuals and eradicate others with negative energy who tend to hinder your efforts. Having confidence in yourself and belief in the skills you possess is key to your ultimate success. Here's the catch, you've got to do the job, that's not going to happen immediately, but it's going to happen!

Introduce yourself with a friendly smile to everyone if you can feel a sense of dread, face it, and do it. It isn't as bad as you thought. Keep your head up and say that you can do this to yourself. Remember to stay reliable. Don't let them see you sweat.

Believe, don't let anyone tell you that you can't do it in everything you do!

You can do anything you think about, and you must believe that! Make it your hobby. Make it your passion.

Confidence is not won. To trust others, they must know that you care. Listen to their challenges. One thing is listening to what is said, while another is listening to what is understood. Be worried about what it says. And let it be between you and them what someone tells you secretly. That's what creates trust.

Crack the Barriers

Every time you notice the knots in your gut are building up, If you feel the knots piling up, take a deep breath, take them one step at a time, analyze the situation, and then create a plan to overcome the fear and keep moving on!! That sense of achievement, if you crack the barriers that once held you back, will always strengthen your faith. Of course, sometimes things won't work. They will learn to see what they are, lessons in life. Take the lessons, learn from them, and then step forward better than ever.

It's never easy to get out and take risks with people you don't know. Also, the most influential people in the world felt some apprehension and fear as they went out of their comfort zone for the first time. The main reason why they succeeded was that they believed in themselves and their ultimate mission and took on their own destiny; THEY MADE IT HAPPEN!!

Then the question is, will you allow your fear of disclosure to govern your fate? Or are you going to look on the face of fear and say, "NOT TODAY?" I know my reply. What are YOURS?

Chapter 8. Build Self Confidence

Confidence is an important part of social skills and nearly impossible to fake convincingly. One way to gain confidence is to know that you have a repertoire of stories that you have told before to good effect and can call upon any time you feel like you don't know what to say.

What is Self Confidence?

Although different people define self-confidence differently, it essentially means believing in oneself.

How we were raised and educated has an impact on our confidence. Others teach us how to think about ourselves and how to act, and these lessons shape our beliefs about ourselves and others. Our experiences and how we've learned to respond to various situations also have an impact on our confidence.

Self-esteem is not a static metric. Our confidence in performing roles and tasks, as well as dealing with situations, can fluctuate, and there will be days we will feel more confident than others.

Lack of self-confidence can be influenced by a lot of factors, including fear of the unknown, criticism, discontentment with one's personal appearance (self-esteem), feeling unprepared, poor time management, a lack of knowledge, and previous failures. When we have no confidence in ourselves, it is often because we are scared of what others will think of us. If we make a mistake, others may laugh at us, complain about us, or make fun of us. Thinking in this manner can prevent us from doing things we want or need to do because we believe the consequences will be too painful or embarrassing.

Overconfidence can be harmful if it leads you to believe that you can do anything, even if you lack the necessary skills, abilities, and knowledge. Overconfidence can result in failure in such situations. Being overconfident also makes you more likely to come across as arrogant or egotistical to others. If you are perceived as arrogant, people are much more likely to take pleasure in your failure.

Although they are frequently linked, confidence and self-esteem are not the same things. We use the term "confidence" to describe how we feel about our ability to perform roles, functions, and tasks. Self-esteem refers to how we perceived ourselves, how we look, how we think - whether or not we believe we are worthy or valued. People with low self-esteem frequently have low confidence, but people with high self-esteem can also have low confidence. It is also possible for people with low self-esteem to be extremely confident in certain areas.

Importance of Having Self Confidence

Brings Your Best Performance When Under Pressure

Sportspeople, artists, and actors are some of the people whose field of work requires a high level of confidence. Those who don't have faith are not likely to make it in this sector. Confidence brings out great performances in people.

Inspiring Others

Those exuding lots of confidence can inspire those around him/her to achieve more. Colleagues are likely to ask for help, and family members also as you are a form of inspiration to them. Your working environment becomes a success.

Enhances Leadership Skills

Leaders are expected to have lots of confidence to address his/her people and accomplish their development projects. A great leader can inspire people for the greater good. This can be accomplished by exuding self-confidence.

People are not likely to follow someone who doesn't believe in himself/herself. The ability to lead is brought by confidence and motivation. They need to show confidence in themselves and the projects they set out to do for society.

Exuding Lots of Constructive Attitudes

Self-confidence enables one's belief to go for greatness and set higher goals. The confidence to aim for more top objectives and greatness.

The Feeling of Appreciation and Respect

It makes you believe in yourself and respect others around you. The same recognition is accorded to you by friends and colleagues due to your personality.

Being Appealing

Most individuals like someone confident about themselves. It's more appealing than someone who lacks self-esteem. They prefer to be in the accompany of a confident person. A partner is likely to be attractive to a potential partner. A study was conducted which targeted relationships between women and men. The attributes one looks for when dating. It was discovered confidence was the most sought-after quality in many of the participants.

Enhances Positive Thoughts

It enables one to reduce self-doubt and set out to do something he/she sets his mind to achieve.

Reduces Anxiety Level and Fear

A confident individual can take high-risk gambles in business that bring high returns as they are comfortable in different sectors.

Action-Oriented and Highly Motivated

Having high-level self-confidence can enable one to be motivated to achieve the goals and visions he has. They are action-oriented and do not only set out plans but take actions to make them a reality.

It Encourages One to Live Your Life for Yourself

The confidence level can be used to define how people see you. People tend to like that person who is confident and give him/her projects as they see it as someone who knows what he/she is doing. Lack of confidence can make you not successful in whatever you were doing or goals. Anxiety and fear are a terrible mix of success.

It Makes People Know That You Love Yourself and Others

Those individuals who lack confidence rely on others to make them feel appreciated. There is no form to sign to be permitted to enjoy yourself and be happy. It's upon you to create happiness for yourself. Having a high level of confidence is more like one's attitude towards something. When the going comes harsh, you become tougher to face your challenges. The efforts you put in will enable you to overcome the tasks at hand. Confidence is a booster in making this become a reality.

Self-Confidence and Positivity

Those that always exhibit a negative attitude are hard to associate with at work or at home. People don't like to be around those that show negative personality and tend to stay away from them. Confident people usually have a positive nature, unlike those that are less confident. They know what they are capable of, and if they set out to achieve something, they will make it work. Those that lack confidence does not believe in themselves and doesn't want to work hard instead of discouraging others with negative comments. They are insecure. When faced with obstacles, they don't try to solve them; instead, they stop there while confident individuals look for better ways to accomplish the task.

Self-Confidence Is a Sign of Maturity

Those with high confidence believe in themselves and don't engage people who try to put them down with negative comments. They are not discouraged easily and have the freedom to do whatever they choose to participate in. 'The principal indication during puberty stage is the act of teenager's expectation, a propensity towards creative work, and a necessity for the strengthening of self-confidence. The teenager unexpectedly shows signs of profoundness to the impoliteness and embarrassments which he/she had beforehand experienced from inactive indifference.'

It's much easier to engage in activities you love when you have a high level of confidence. Prosperity and success come to those who can manage to control their self-esteem and fear. When your working environment is toxic, one can engage in hobbies that can help them reduce stress levels. Fear and anxiety can be easily controlled if one decides to use the above techniques, as discussed.

Here are some tricks to help you build self-confidence.

35: How To Fake It 'Til You Make It

You've probably heard this saying from time to time, but the science exists that suggests that *acting* a certain way is one of the best ways to *become* a certain way. In other words, if you pretend to be confident, then you will actually become confident.

In psychology and neuroscience, this is known as the Hebbian Principle. How it works is that when a human being does something, which can literally be anything, the tiny neural circuits in their brain light up and start firing to make the "thing" happen. Say you want to lift your right arm up right now. You think about it, and those circuits start firing to make it happen, sending the signals for your body to lift your arm. Now, you can resist doing it if you really want, but how aware of your arm are you right now?

If you're to lift your arm, then the message sent becomes a "link," and the more you allow this link to happen, the easier it becomes. The human brain likes the easy life, and this is why so many of us have habits. We've made the same habit over and over again so often that we do it without thinking, so the brain saves energy and just "does," rather than spending all its time thinking.

Still with me?

Now, we've evolved so far up to this point that you can actually trick this system into developing new habits or, in this case, entirely new states of mind by purely thinking about doing something. Let's keep it related to confidence.

If you were to get up in the morning, go to the mirror, and act like your most confident self, portraying the level of confidence you want yourself to have, and actively act out how you would be (yes, this means talking to yourself out loud), then over time, you would naturally become more confident because you're firing up those circuits saying that you want to be more confident, and then carrying out that command.

You're actively hard-wiring your brain. It's such a clever technique.

This is why motivational speakers will jump up and down and build up their energy before going on stage. Popular speaker Tony Robbins actually has a mini-trampoline he jumps on just moments before heading in front of the crowd. It's to build up his energy and get his blood flowing, so when it comes to showing time, he's already in the high-energy state of mind he needs to be in to deliver.

You can do the same!

Basically, define the type of person you want to be and what level of confidence you want to have, practice it in your free time, and then start to implement this level of confidence naturally in your interactions, and you'll notice an incredible difference! Here are some tips that are helpful to make it.

- Watch movies and TV shows and see what kind of people you resonate with to define your style of confidence

- Do the same with people in your life

- Practice in front of the mirror for five minutes every single day

- Experiment with different styles of confidence

- Apply your practices to everyday situations you find yourself in

36: How To Overcome Thoughts That Hold You Back

Thoughts that stop you from living the life you want to live and hold you back are known as limiting beliefs, and these are crushing your confidence.

Imagine you're going into a job interview, and you're feeling so nervous. You can't help but think you're going to mess everything up, and you keep playing through all the various negative ways the meeting could go. If you're focusing on the bad stuff, then how can you expect to be confident going forward? You're definitely not going to be your best self.

The way to get around this problem is to become aware of what your limiting beliefs are. You can do this long-term through journaling, meditation, counseling, and doing everything we talked about in the first chapter regarding developing your sense of self. However, there is something that we can do right now, and it's a fun little exercise I love.

A Quick Little Exercise

Grab a pen and paper and imagine you are going to meet with someone for the first time.

That could be a new client, a stranger in a cafe or on the street, or you're heading into an unfamiliar situation where you need to talk to people, but you don't really know them very well, if at all.

Take a moment to imagine it clearly, and now write down all the negative thoughts that come up. Do you think these people will think you're weird or annoying? Are you conscious of your physical appearance? Are you worried that they won't like you or will talk down to you? Write down anything that comes to mind.

When you read them back, these are your limiting beliefs and things you're going to need to work on when it comes to becoming confident. These are the thoughts that will hold you back and stop you from reaching your full potential. Of course, there's an infinite number of thoughts that could come up here, and it will take time to work through them all, but fortunately, there are tons of articles, books, and websites that can help you address your issues.

For me, I thought people would believe I didn't know what I was talking about, and I wasn't qualified to share my experience because I was still young. After some research, I discovered this is a state of mind called Imposter Syndrome, and I was able to take steps to work on letting these limiting thoughts go.

While a little unrelated, I found this limiting beliefs discovery technique very fun when it comes to looking at your finances. Now get your paper and pen again and write down your dream wage you'd like to earn in a year. Now add a zero to the end (the right-hand side end) and write down all the reasons why you can't earn that amount. These are your limiting beliefs, and it can be incredibly interesting to see what comes up!

37: How To Adopt Confident Body Language

A leading Harvard psychologist, Amy Cuddy, looked into body language and how the way we act physically affects our mindset, state of mind, and overall confidence. In her studies, she took 42 men and women and had them perform what is known as low and high power poses.

These basically pose that show how confident someone is. In other words, the stereotypical view of a shy person is crouched over and small, hunched, as though trying to hide and not be noticed. On the other hand, a power poses beaming confidence would be something like the Superman pose, with hands-on-hips and their head held high.

In the study, the participants were asked to hold certain poses for two minutes, and then saliva samples were taken.

The results were clear. Those people who had adopted high-power poses, similar to the Superman pose, showed lower cortisol levels (the stress hormone) and increased testosterone levels—both of which indicate the person was more relaxed, more confident, less stressed, and more willing to take rests. And this was all just for adopting a different pose.

Hand in hand with faking it until you're making it. You can feel the effects right now. Assuming you're reading this sitting down, straighten your back, and sit back with your hands behind your head, more commonly referred to as the "President's Pose." It looks like the classic office desk pose where you've completed a sale and cross your legs up on the desk because you're so happy with what you've just achieved, although having your legs on the desk is optional.

Have strength in your pose, widen your chest, and do a pose that reminds you of feeling proud. All the stereotypical poses that come to mind will do. Hold the pose for 30 seconds to a minute. How do you feel? How confident and ready to take on the world does it make you feel? This is just how powerful such a simple act can be. Practice these poses when going into tense situations to become far more confident than you would normally be!

38: How To Get Hands-On

Hand in hand with the point above, using your hands as your main expressive form of body language can be a great way to feel, look, and become confident. Research by Carol Kinsey Gorman found that listeners will have a much more positive connection with public speakers who gesture with their hands to exaggerate and communicate their points.

The same works the other way around too. If you're playing with your hair, fiddling with your sleeves or your clothes, or keeping your hands still in between your legs while sitting, this can convey the image that you're nervous or anxious. Take control of your hands and channel your inner energy for whatever topic you're talking about!

39: How To Implement Eye Contact

Being able to hold and maintain eye contact is pretty much the cornerstone of confidence. If you look away from someone when they're talking to you, look at the ground, or basically anywhere other than you, then it just oozes a lack of confidence. When someone is ashamed of something they've done, they look at the ground because they can't bring themselves to make eye contact. Even dogs do this!

A Texan study held back in 2013 found that people on average make eye contact between 30 and 60% of the time, but if you're looking to make an emotional connection with someone, then you're going to need to up this to about 60–70% of the time. And it's not easy.

If you're consciously thinking about making eye contact with someone for a longer-than-normal period of time, but it's not something you're used to, then chances are, you're going to feel uncomfortable and maybe even as though you're staring. This will make you nervous, and the whole confidence thing starts to fall apart.

However, there are some tips you can follow to make it easy, and also remember, practice makes perfect, so keep trying!

Firstly, you don't need to lock your eyes on both of the eyes of the other person, but instead, focus on one eye. This may sound a little strange, but it works. If you're still feeling uncomfortable, try looking at their eyebrows. Don't look higher than this or lower than their eye level because it will just feel weird, as though you're not paying full attention. Eyebrows are fine. Practice with yourself in the mirror for better results.

When you're coupling this tip with the others, we've been speaking about throughout this book. Then you should find yourself naturally being able to make eye contact more and more. Do not stop practicing, and you will see the results.

40: How To Slow Down

It's a common trait that people will speak quickly when they are nervous, and this is especially prevalent with people who are new to public speaking. The idea is that someone speaks as fast as possible so they can finish what they're saying quickly and then no longer have to talk. However, this is a clear sign you're both nervous and anxious, not only showing this to the other person but also validating your fears with yourself.

The simple solution is to slow down. Consciously slow down the speed at which you're talking.

I'm not saying go monotone and drag everything on, but find a nice pace you're comfortable with (which you can find practicing in the mirror!), and then when you're nervous and find yourself speeding up, you can mindfully slow yourself back down. Research shows that around 190 words per minute are the ideal speaking speed for being comfortable and sending across your message effectively.

Chapter 9. The Touch of Genuine Compliment

Suppose you are talking to a coworker who recently and successfully completed a work project. You congratulate him by saying something along the lines of "Great job on the Johnson project." Your coworker mumbles a thank you and goes on about his business. This probably wasn't the response you were expecting. Later on, while getting a drink with some coworkers, you compliment a particularly attractive coworker with, "You really are very pretty." She tenses and looks nervous, then excuses herself from the conversation. What went wrong?

We've seen how people enjoy talking about themselves, and we've learned a few ways to ask questions to give them the opportunity to do so. But what happens when a lull in the conversation stalls any attempt to keep them talking? What if your compliment is met with indifference? What if you sense nervousness in them? How do you counteract their anxiety?

Everyone likes to receive a genuine compliment. But, if given the wrong way, a compliment can serve to make a person feel indifferent, uncomfortable, or even embarrassed.

How do you avoid this? Keep these tricks in mind.

41: How TO Avoid Flattery-Be Sincere

Your compliments won't be believed or accepted if they aren't seen to be sincere. A genuine compliment comes from the heart and is intended to make the recipient feel good about themselves, not simply serve as a means to continue a conversation. You want people to open up to you, not to talk for the sake of talking.

Something else to avoid is complimenting someone with the hopes of receiving a compliment in return. If you don't genuinely admire something about someone, it's best to keep a compliment to yourself rather than have that person think you are insincere. Flattery and brown-nosing are not admirable traits in anyone and will only serve to make other people think you are self-serving.

☒ Be specific. In the first example above, the project coworker got a compliment he had likely heard a hundred times over. When congratulating or complimenting someone, say what in particular about them or their actions you like. A better compliment would have been "I like how you handled the client's concerns" or "You did a great job addressing the budget issue."

☒ Be appropriate. In the second example, the attractive coworker found the direct compliment about her looks creepy and unnerving. Comments about another person's appearance can very often be construed as an attempt to be romantic, which will cause problems if you don't mean your remark to be taken as such. Even if you are romantically interested in someone, there are better ways to express this. Until you know a person better, avoid complimenting their physical traits, or at least keep your compliments specific and brief. "You have a great smile" would work better in this scenario. Remember that even if what you are saying is positive, it is still a judgment, and no one likes being judged.

⊠   Know when to let it go. Do not expect your compliments to be accepted every time or expect them to be returned. If a compliment falls flat, simply move on with the conversation; trying to "fix" the situation will only make it more awkward. If you receive a compliment, accept it graciously with a "Thank you, you are kind to say so" and move on, but don't match their compliment with one of your own. Remember--you want to be sincere.

42: How NOT TO EXAGGERATE.

You may think that a hyperbolized compliment seems more sincere, but it doesn't. Instead of something like "That's the most beautiful cake I've ever seen," try "The cake you decorated looks really beautiful. I can tell you worked hard on it."

43: How TO Find Out What They Like About Themselves

People are mirrors. Anything you like or do not like about someone reflects something you like or do not like about yourself. One reason compliments fall flat is that they can touch on people's insecurities. If someone tells you you have a great figure and you've struggled with your weight your entire life, you may be **more** self-conscious rather than less. You may not know what another person's insecurities are, but those aren't important; make an effort to find out what their favorite attributes are and focus on those.

Finding out what a person likes about themselves is as simple as listening to them. While talking to someone, if they spend a while talking about something important to them, you can often learn something about them you can use in a compliment: their work ethic, generosity, intelligence, and so on. For example, if your neighbor is talking about training for a marathon, they probably like being physically fit. A good compliment would be, "You really take great care of yourself. I admire your dedication to being healthy."

If you still can't glean a person's strengths by listening, there's nothing wrong with asking if you approach it the right way. Simply asking someone, "What is your favorite thing about yourself?" may meet with self-consciousness, especially if they are shy and insecure by nature. A less direct question, like "What is your favorite attribute in people?" gives them the option to say what things they like in other people that they may share, even if they don't realize it. When they answer, compliment them on that attribute if they share it. For example, if they say kindness is their favorite attribute, you can say (as long as you mean it, of course), "I can see that you are a very nice person yourself." Another way to phrase this would be, "What is something you have always admired in other people?"

44: How TO Eliminate Their Self - Doubt OF Your Goal

Everybody has their strengths and weaknesses. But all too often, we focus on negativity and bad experiences. How do we find the strengths in others? It's hard to find something to compliment when all you focus on is negativity; dismiss your negative thoughts when you're getting to know someone. It may be that you find you really don't like a person after spending time talking to them, and that's ok. Otherwise, if you do enjoy someone's company, you obviously already see their positive aspects. You just need to put them to work.

Pay attention to what makes them smile. The more you get to know a person, the more you will see their passions and motives come out in day-to-day moments. Remember to use these moments to pay genuine compliments when appropriate, especially if you can see they feel insecure or have a tough day. A person who laughs a lot would appreciate a compliment along the lines of "You have an amazing sense of humor." An animal lover would like to hear, "You are a warm, caring person."

Remember, you are focusing on the person's strengths and positive attributes. Sometimes you just have to remind them that they're there.

Let's see this in action. Suppose you are talking to your neighbor, and she mentions she's been working on her novel. You know this neighbor well enough to know she is creative and intelligent, so you take the opportunity to compliment her, saying something like, "That's incredible! I'm sure it will be great when you finish it." Anyone who has ever written knows how difficult putting words to paper can be, so your compliment will likely mean a lot. Later on, if she mentions how difficult writing is or talks about having writer's block, you can say (and mean it), "If anyone can do it, you can. You are very clever and creative." Saying that will remove your neighbor's self-doubt and motivate her to work harder.

Some people can't take a compliment. No matter what you say to them, they only see the negative. You tell them they are a great musician, and they focus on how much practice they need. You compliment their cooking, and they insist they simply followed a recipe and have no natural talent in the kitchen. The best way to handle such negativity is to smile and say, "I mean it just the same." Once they see your compliment is indeed from the heart, they will begin to accept it and believe more in their own abilities and strengths.

Chapter 10. Have Magnetic Personality

Anywhere you go, there always seems to be someone, or perhaps a few people, who are surrounded. People gravitate to them, want to talk to them, want to hear what they have to say. Being on the outside and looking in, it is easy to think they are "magical" or have something you don't have.

The truth is, anyone can learn to draw people towards them. By now, you have the skills to strike up a conversation with anyone; now, it's time to learn how to make people want to talk to **you**. Whenever you see a new person, there is something about them that makes you want to meet them. At a social gathering, you may be drawn toward someone who has an infectious laugh, an easy and confident manner of speaking, or they may seem to make people around them happy. Not everyone is born with a magnetic personality, but anyone can learn to develop one.

Here are some tricks you can use and apply.

45: How To Have A Positive Attitude

Have you ever had a coworker who had nothing good to say ever? His boss is always treating him unfairly. His coworkers disrespect him, he can't stay on top of his bills, his girlfriend left him, his dog bit him. Any solution or encouragement you offer is met with indifference or more negativity. To him, everything is pointless. How long did it take for you to get bored and weary of the conversation?

No one likes negativity. True, not every experience or interaction you ever have is going to be positive, but it's **focusing** on negativity that turns people off. Focusing on negativity makes you look self-absorbed. The depressing coworker above that talks exclusively about what's going wrong in his life doesn't want a conversation so much as he wants a sounding board for his frustration. If you've ever talked to anyone like that, you know that it gets old very quickly.

So how can you be more positive? Can you replace every unpleasant thought in your head with a happy one? Of course not. The key to having a positive attitude is not to avoid having negative thoughts and experiences but to know how to process those thoughts and experiences constructively. Here's an example: You make a mistake at work which leads to a disciplinary meeting and a stern lecture from a superior. Do you focus on how unfair the meeting was? How dumb must you have been to make such a mistake? Or do you look at the situation as a learning experience, focus on improving your performance, and move forward? If a coworker asks you later on what happened, how do you respond?

A part of having a positive attitude is taking responsibility for yourself and your actions. A negative person has things happen to them. A positive person **makes** things happen. In the example above, when your coworker asks what happened, you can blame the situation, a lack of proper training, or say that your boss is out to get you. You will look like you are trying to shift responsibility for your error onto someone else. If, on the other hand, you accept that you made a mistake and focus on learning from the incident, you will look mature and responsible. Everyone makes mistakes, including the hypothetical boss and coworker in this scenario. You will seem more confident and positive if you accept responsibility and move forward. Here are some more tips on maintaining a positive attitude:

☒ Be enthusiastic. Be eager to meet new people. Get excited about events and projects. You will find that people will gravitate to you and want to share your enthusiasm.

☒ Maintain inner peace. Positivity comes from within. A healthy self-esteem will give you a confident, happy vibe that others will find irresistible.

☒ Be interested. Be curious about others, and want to hear what they have to say.

☒ Look for the best in others. When you look for the best in people, you make them want to be their best.

46: How To Have Humor

The first thing many people think of when they hear the word "humor" is something, like a joke or story, that was designed to be funny, to make people laugh. Certainly, it never hurts you to have a few jokes in mind when talking to people, as long as you keep them appropriate to your audience. Clean, family-friendly jokes are always appropriate, so save your edgier jokes for when you know your audience better. Here are some more tips on developing a good sense of humor.

☒ Be witty. Sarcasm has a certain humorous appeal but focuses on negativity. Wit, on the other hand, focuses on being clever and funny in any everyday situation. It can be a difficult skill to learn. Watch comedians, and pay attention to their timing and delivery. Always remember that a large part of being witty is spontaneity. If being spontaneous is difficult for you, practice making jokes and witty observations with a friend.

☒ What makes you laugh? If you find something funny, chances are at least some other people will as well. Remember jokes and witticisms that make you laugh, and repeat them to others--when they are appropriate, of course. You wouldn't tell a sexually explicit joke at a church function, you wouldn't tell a "dumb blonde" joke to a blonde, and you shouldn't repeat racist jokes anywhere.

☒ Know when to let it go. Not every joke you crack is going to be met with raucous laughter. Sometimes, for whatever reason, a joke will fall flat. Sometimes you can recover, sometimes you can't. If a witty observation doesn't gain applause, you think it should just move on. Try the joke with a different audience if you can, or just chalk it up to being less-than-clever.

There is a saying: "Blessed are those who can laugh at themselves, for they shall never cease to be amused." Having a good sense of humor is not confined to knowing a few jokes; you must also be able to see the humor in everyday situations and not take yourself too seriously. There will be times when you need to let go of your pride and acknowledge your own faults. No one is infallible, and knowing how to laugh at yourself can not only make you more likable but does wonders for your self-esteem.

47: How To Appear More Intelligent Than Others

Everyone has their own brand of intelligence. Some people have "book smarts," a formal education focused on facts and figures. Some people have "street smarts," a common-sense gained from experience rather than studying. Some people have a so-called sixth sense or natural intuition. Some people know how to say the right thing at the right time, and some are creative, some are analytical. In other words, no one is "dumb" in the common sense of the word. Everyone, yourself included, has something to offer the world.

What makes people seem dull or unintelligent is not their lack of knowledge but more of a lack of opportunity to exhibit their knowledge and (b) not knowing how to exhibit their knowledge. You may hold a doctorate in molecular biology, but at a poetry reading, you will likely not have much to say. Obviously, you aren't foolish, but you don't have the proper platform to show what you know.

But fear not. With a little practice, you can look intelligent to any group and in any setting, which will gain you opportunities to share your strengths. Here are some tips on how to achieve this:

☒ Using big words only helps if you know how to use them. If you cannot accurately define or say the word "incorrigible," you shouldn't use it in a sentence. Someone who **does** know what the word means will catch that you are trying to use big words to seem smarter. Once you learn the meaning of "incorrigible" (not able to be corrected or reformed) and how to properly use it, you will fare better.

☒ Speak clearly, not loudly. A common misconception is if you talk loud, you will seem smart. You will only seem loud. Instead, speak clearly and at a regular pace.

☒ Again, listen and be curious. This is another instance in which seeming genuinely interested in others helps you. In this case, you seem smarter by seeming naturally curious.

☒ Explore your natural intelligence. Intelligence essentially knows things. You may read more about the things that you are interested to learn. If you are an art lover, go to art museums. If you love nature, try natural history museums and nature trails. You'll become smarter and have fun in the process.

☒ Look the part. Taking care of your appearance makes you look more confident and intelligent. You don't need to wear an evening gown or tuxedo for every event, but simply wear neat, well-fitting clothes and maintain proper personal hygiene. Keep your hair and nails neatly groomed. Wear makeup if you like, but don't bother if you don't enjoy it--it will feel, and look, like a mask and only serve to make you feel less confident.

You have likely noticed a pattern--many of the tips you've seen involve being confident and listening well to others. This is not meant to be repetitive. An air of confidence and the ability to get people to talk will cause people to gravitate to you, to want to hear what you have to say. Remember: you are important, you have value, and you have something to say. Even if you don't make friends out of every person you meet, people respect self-esteem.

Chapter 11. Develop Meaningful Relationships

And here we are. We've arrived at the final part of this book. As you can see, the final title of this book reads "Developing Meaningful Relationships," but so far, we've spent all our time on conversations and being able to talk to anyone about anything, which you should be able to do by now. However, the last question that remains is simple.

How can you go from knowing someone and wowing them with your charm, confidence, and small talk, and then actually develop a proper relationship with them? How can you meet people and become true friends with them?

It's a weird thought that so many of us are becoming more and more disconnected in a world that's more hyper-connected than ever before. I can't remember entirely, but when I was a kid back in school, it seemed like making friends was so easy. Sure, you wouldn't get along or like the company of everyone (it would be weird if you did), but there were no inhibitions in talking to new people. You would just chat about whatever was going on, and if you got along, you became friends.

It feels like there's an underlying level of pressure and anxiety that stops things today from being that easy. It's a cringe thought to imagine walking up to someone and just talking to them and then becoming lifelong friends. Maybe in an ideal world, right? Maybe you believe that logic only works in the movies? It's not. To see what life can alternatively be like t just takes some effort and time.

Taking everything you know so far, how can you go from meeting someone for the first time, small talking with them, telling them stories, charming them with your charisma and confidence, and then ultimately becoming friends with them, or at least developing a meaningful relationship of some kind?

In this chapter, you will learn how to develop meaningful relationships.

The Benefits are Unparalleled

While having strong connections with people in your life and talking to lots of people is definitely going to make you feel less lonely and more charismatic and confident, having a million acquaintances is no substitute for having five friends that you have a deep and meaningful connection.

Research shows that having proper connections with people can bring so many benefits into your life; it's hard to know where to begin. A 2014 study carried out by the Society for Personality, and Social Psychology, found that meaningful relationships will:

- Help you live longer
- Improves many aspects of your mental health

- Improves your ability to judge your own well-being
- Increases your self-confidence
- Provides you with wide perspectives
- Provides you with increased resilience in most aspects of your life

There are even sources that claim that having meaningful relationships is "the healthiest thing you can do for yourself" (Medical Daily, 2014). In other words, focus on developing meaningful relationships. This will bring so much goodness into your life.

To make and develop a meaningful relationship with others, you can use the following tricks:

49: How To Understand The Barriers

To fully understand how to make close friends, you need to know the things that are holding you back. The two main culprits of this are:

- Technology ruining our attention span, make it harder to concentrate, and emulates the feeling of being connected to those we love and care about
- Having busy lives, such as working full-time jobs, working on side projects, and trying to keep up with the fast-paced life that feels common, as promoted by the "mainstream" way of living.

In other words, just because you see your best friend's name on your Facebook feed, that doesn't mean you're actually connecting with them. You need to put your phone down and reach out to them properly and make time to have actual experiences with them, but more on that in a bit.

Now we're going to explore how to take these initial relationships in your life and move forward, forming stronger bonds than ever before and being able to connect with these people that you might one day say you love.

50: How You Can't Be Friends With Everyone

Before we really get into the tips, make sure you're aware of the fact that you're not going to be friends with everyone, and nor should you try to be.

I'm not saying you should outwardly be blunt and forceful to people you don't like. Stay civil. Instead, if you really feel a natural draw to someone, and you feel a connection is there, then it's definitely something you should pursue. If not, that doesn't matter. You're just a step closer to finding the people who are right in your life.

51: How To Spend Time With Your New Friends

As I write this book, the world has been gripped by the COVID-19 pandemic, and it's mixed up the world in ways that we could have never predicted. This has made many of us become more disconnected due to lockdown rules, but the happiest people were the ones who still found a way to connect and spend time together.

If you want to connect with someone and deepen your relationship with them, you need to spend time with them, create memories together, and be in each other's presence, not just online. It's clear that times like the COVID-19 pandemic means that connecting in such an intimate way isn't always possible, but that doesn't mean dedicating time to each other is any less essential.

Whether you're going for a socially distanced walk, hosting online activities like Zoom quiz nights or group Netflix streams, or even just chatting via a video call, spending time with people is a must. Dedicating time to each other (and making sure it's fair both ways) is how relationships grow.

Support Each Other

The latest research shows that friends become closer than ever when they help each other through hard times. This doesn't just mean dealing with a tragedy or trauma, but instead could just be offering support on a friend's self-improvement journey. It's always easier and more effective to go through change with someone by your side.

In a 2008 study, researchers placed some participants at the top of a hill either alone, alongside a stranger, or standing next to a friend. When asked to grade how steep the hill was, the participants who were next to a friend thought the hill to be far less steep than those who were standing alone. In other words, when you're standing with someone you're connected to, the hard times aren't so bad.

Finally, and perhaps most importantly, be yourself around those you love.

It can be hard sometimes to even acknowledge we're wearing masks around those we love, let alone trying to take them off, but it's never been more important to embrace who you are and just be you.

If you're pretending to be someone you're not with your friends, then eventually, it's going to backfire. Either you won't be happy or your friends won't, so save yourself the drama and just be unapologetically you. Even if you change over time (which everyone does), real friends will be accepting of exactly who you are.

And that's it! If you can follow these simple tricks and tips, you'll be able to take the people you know and like in your life and turn them into friends that you share a deep, meaningful connection, and the world becomes your oyster.

Conclusion

You have come so far to reach this part of the book. Congratulations!

Social anxiety is quite a common issue, but there is no reason to allow it to control your life. Socializing, making friends, getting to know and understand others--these are some of life's simplest pleasures. Whether your aim is to have a large circle of acquaintances, or just a few close friends, to rise to the top of your career or become more effective in your current role; the ability to communicate effectively, to understand the wants and needs of others and cause them to see your own point of view, and even influence them, is essential.

Small talk is just what it sounds like--a conversation about unimportant matters or current events. Some topics may include the weather, current events, sports, or work. There are some people who dislike and avoid small talk, but you can use it as a tool to learn about and gain rapport with others, and to let others get to know you. There is an art to it, however. You should be careful of talking for too long or dominating the conversation, or you may come off as self-absorbed and inconsiderate. Also, your topic of discussion should be appropriate for the setting and for who you are talking to. Always know what topics are open to discussion and which topics to stay away from.

After reading this book, you should have a good understanding of how to socialize with others. But knowing how to carry on a conversation is only the beginning--now it's time to practice your new skills. The next time you are at a party and see someone you would like to know better, step out of the corner and break the ice. Use your small talk skills to get a feel for their personality. Ask questions. Listen. Find common ground. Make them feel good about who they are. The more you socialize, the better you get at it, and the more interesting you become. You may have a few missteps and awkward moments, but use these moments as learning experiences, and you will find that, before long, other people will gravitate to you and want to hear what **you** have to say.

When it comes to making a change in your life, these are the three essential elements you're going to need to focus on:

Education. Awareness. Practice.

You need knowledge and information so you know what decisions you're going to make. You need awareness to apply everything you've learned, to recognize where you go wrong, what you do right, and to be aware of where you need to get better. You need to keep practicing to get better.

And so, we come to the end of our journey, and it's all over to you!

I hope you've enjoyed reading this more than anything, and you've learned a lot. I know I said I was going to say it one last time chapters ago, but here's another for good measure: Don't give up on your learning path! The path to better conversation and communication, like all self-improvement journeys, is a continuous learning curve with an infinite skill cap. Don't let social anxiety and fears hold you back. Open up, engage with others and build meaningful relationships.

As said, the only way you're going to do this is by practicing over and over again, being willing to embrace any fears or anxieties you may have in order to overcome them. Just keep at it, take everything we've spoken about with baby steps, and you'll see big improvements in no time at all!

I would love to hear some feedback from you! Whenever you bought the book, hit me up with a review and a few words letting me know what you thought about the book, what you liked, and what you think I could do better.

I'm only a human being doing what I love, but I'm always striving to be better and to give you the best experience I can! I also love hearing all the amazing ways these books help you see life in a different way, so let me know and inspire me to keep going!

References

(n.d.). From Skills You Need: https://www.skillsyouneed.com/ips/listening-skills.html

(n.d.). From Psychology Today: https://www.psychologytoday.com/us/basics/humor

(n.d.). From https://www.improveyoursocialskills.com/how-to-make-eye-contact

Body Language: What's Really Behind a Smile? (2014, March 11). From Womens Health: https://www.womenshealthmag.com/life/a19982102/meaning-of-a-smile/

Building and sustaining Relationship. (n.d.). From Community Tool Box: https://ctb.ku.edu/en/table-of-contents/leadership/leadership-functions/build-sustain-relationships/main

Burton, N. (2012, May 30). From psychology today: https://www.psychologytoday.com/us/blog/hide-and-seek/201205/building-confidence-and-self-esteem

Economy, P. (n.d.). *9 Ways to Make a Great First Impression.* From INc: https://www.inc.com/peter-economy/9-ways-to-make-a-great-first-impression.html

How to Be the Most Interesting (& Interested) Person in the Room. (2021, March 26). From eschool of thought: https://eschoolofthought.com/blog/f/how-to-be-the-most-interesting-interested-person-in-the-room?blogcategory=Building+Marketable+Skills

Ifould, R. (2015, November 28). *How to talk to anyone: the experts' guide*. From The Guardian: https://www.theguardian.com/lifeandstyle/2015/nov/28/how-to-talk-to-anyone-the-experts-guide

Indeed Editorial Team. (2021, February 19). *10 Ways To Develop Your Social Skills* . From Indeed: https://www.indeed.com/career-advice/career-development/developing-social-skills

Kashyap, S. (n.d.). *Here's How Effective Communication is in the Hands of 73% of Professionals*. From Proof HUb: https://www.proofhub.com/articles/effective-communication

Ma, L. (2011, Jull 12). *10 Tips to Talk About Anything With Anyone*. From Psychology Today: https://www.psychologytoday.com/us/blog/fulfillment-any-age/201107/10-tips-talk-about-anything-anyone

Mooney, L. (n.d.). *Qualities of a Magnetic Personality*. From az central: https://yourbusiness.azcentral.com/10-qualities-magnetic-personality-11157.html

Morin, A. (2020, April 27). From verywell mind: https://www.verywellmind.com/how-to-boost-your-self-confidence-4163098

Morin, D. (2019, February 13). *How to Improve Your Conversation Skills*. From Social Pro: https://socialpronow.com/blog/improve-conversation-skills/

Natasha. (2019, April 29). *TIPS FOR HOW TO GIVE GENUINE COMPLIMENTS & UNIQUE COMPLIMENTS TO GIVE SOMEONE*. From The artisan Life: https://natashalh.com/unique-compliments-give-someone/

Nordquist, R. (2020, June 29). *What Is Nonverbal Communication?* From Thought Co.: https://www.thoughtco.com/what-is-nonverbal-communication-1691351

Paler, J. (2019, January 7). *How to overcome social anxiety: 5 simple steps*. From Hack Spirit: https://hackspirit.com/how-to-overcome-social-anxiety-5-simple-steps/#:~:text=How%20to%20overcome%20social%20anxiety%3A%205%20simple%20steps,your%20breathing.%20...%205%20Face%20your%20fears.%20

Quast, L. (2013, September 9). *5 Tips To Create A Positive First Impression*. From Forbes: https://www.forbes.com/sites/lisaquast/2013/09/09/5-tips-to-create-a-positive-first-impression/

Rampton, J. (2015, January 13). *25 Tips for Having Meaningful Relationships*. From Entrepreneur Asia: https://www.entrepreneur.com/article/241217

Vanessa. (n.d.). *The Science of succeding with People*. From Science Of People: https://www.scienceofpeople.com/

Book - 2

15 Social Practices of Saying the Right Thing in any Situation

Effective Small Talk for Improve Your Social Skills to Start a meaningful Conversation and Talk to Anyone without Shyness & Anxiety

INTRODUCTION

Small talk is casual because it is the first stepping stone to... "serious talk." Asking questions that you don't want to be answered, such as, how are you? It facilitates interaction for both parties and forms the basis for developing a real connection. It serves for the formation of confidence.

The purpose of talking to other people is to get what we want from them. So if your goal is to have a more meaningful conversation, unfortunately, you will have to go through the small talk first. But it is not easy to go from one to the other. We can instantly identify when something feels "heavy" or "deep" because it is out of our expectations; it is not an everyday experience to have a meaningful conversation with someone.

Small talk is like driving in first gear. It's going to advance you, but it won't get you very far. Depending on your environment, the discomfort of casual conversation can be very different. It can be easier to handle at parties because you go with the expectation of making social connections. You don't walk out of your gym class —sweaty, half-dead—expecting that you will meet a handsome boy/girl you used to go to school with. In this context, there is pressure to cut off the interaction because it is not naturally social. However, this is when you will gain a greater sense of satisfaction if you try to go beyond the empty talk.

You're walking through the supermarket, looking like a run-over animal, when you suddenly bump into that person, you added to Facebook, or Instagram or Snapchat when you were in high gear at a party. You do not remember his/her name, but he/she recognizes you and comes to you. Now you must prepare yourself for the most casual of the world's small talk. It's going to be horrible.

Despite constantly evolving social expectations, one thing that hasn't changed is the awkwardness of small talk. Social media may have broken down the barriers between individuals, but with increased trust online comes increased anxiety in real life. You might feel relaxed when you send a direct message to someone on Facebook, WhatsApp, or Twitter, but what if you see them in person? No way would you be that kind of idiot.

We understand you. Perhaps, you think that you are the only one that is like that. You believe that you cannot get ahead because you made many attempts and were not successful. You can even think that you are condemned to suffer countless embarrassments throughout your life. You are not alone.

The right phrase depends entirely on your goal, what you want from this particular person. Do you want a closer relationship? Make more direct eye contact and mention his/her name a lot. Most people will get more involved, almost immediately, if you mention their name in a sentence. Mimicking their body language is also helpful.

But maybe things have gotten out of hand, and you find someone you saw a lot (an ex-lover/best friend) but hoped you wouldn't see again. In this case, you can end the encounter by making less eye contact, using a calmer tone of voice, making more closed gestures, and crossing your arms at chest level.

So, whether you like it or not, small talk is the lubricant of social relationships, even at work. Those moments of chatting while taking coffee or before a meeting play an essential role in professional success. They allow you to integrate more readily into a new company, expand your network of contacts, or create a more relaxed atmosphere.

The art of small talk lies in knowing how to detect the limits of your interlocutor. It also determines if a topic could be considered uncomfortable or out of place. To avoid taking risks, tackle classic (and not too emotional) topics that work in any situation: sports, movies, series, travel, cooking, or only the latest news.

For this reason, you will see in this book how you should handle small talk. Not only will we teach you the most critical steps, but you will also see the keys to breaking the ice at work and with your teammates. You will also avoid the endless chatter about time, which only serves to break the silence and does not allow you to demonstrate your intelligence.

Suppose you are the kind of person who ever experienced those seconds of panic when you meet him/her, from accounting, in the elevator. He/she looks at you, you look at him/her, you both know you have nothing interesting to say, but the silence becomes more and more unbearable; this book is for you.

Take some of your time to read this book. You will learn many things that will serve you in each of your encounters in which you have to be brilliant, not shy.

Enjoy it!

Chapter 1. The Basics of Small Talk

Often, we have dialogues about unimportant topics, trivialities that do not matter to us at all but that serve to talk with neighbors or start conversations with strangers. Could the topic be the least of it, and what is important is what we tell ourselves with body language? They are called small-talk. So, now, the question is the following:

What Is Small Talk?

It is part of the ritual of approaching the other. It is a way of preparing the ground to later deal with more critical issues. Or to maintain pleasant contact with the neighbors, the bartender, the grocer, even if we are never going to see them again. It has to see with seduction because by addressing a person under the pretext of any trivial subject, you tell him/her that he/she is essential for you.

In particular, it helps new acquaintances to explore and categorize the social position of others. Small talk is closely related to people's need to maintain a cheerful face and feel approved by those who listen. Lubricates social interactions in a very flexible way, but the desired role often depends on where in the conversation, the little talk occurs. So, Small talk relies on the following three points.

Conversation Opener: When speakers don't know each other, it allows them to show that they have friendly intentions and desire some kind of positive interaction. A business meeting will enable people to establish the reputation and level of expertise of others. If there is already a relationship between the two interlocutors, your small talk serves as a gentle introduction before engaging in more active conversation topics. It allows them to point out their mood and feel the other person's perspective.

Suddenly, ending an exchange can seem like you are rejecting the other person at the end of a conversation. Small talk can be used to mitigate that rejection, affirm the relationship between the two people, and smooth the separation.

Filling spaces to avoid silence: In many cultures, silences between two people are often considered uncomfortable or uncomfortable. Tension can be reduced by initiating the phatic conversation until a more substantial topic comes up. In general, humans find prolonged silence painful and sometimes unbearable. That may be due to human evolutionary history as a social species, as in many other social animals, silence is a communicative sign of potential danger.

In some conversations, there is no specific functional or informational element. The following example of small talk is between two colleagues passing each other in a hallway:

- James: Hi, Peter.

- Peter: Oh! Hi James, how are you?
- James: Good, thank you. Have a good day?
- Peter: Yes, thank you. See you tomorrow.
- James: OK, see you.

In that example, the phatic talk elements at the beginning and end of the conversation have been merged. The whole short conversation fills the space. This type of speech is often called talk.

The need to use small talk depends on the relationship between the people who have a conversation. Couples in an intimate relationship can indicate their level of closeness by the lack of small talk. They can comfortably accept silence in circumstances that would be uncomfortable for two people who were only casual friends.

In work situations, small talk tends to occur primarily between peer workers, but managers can use it to develop working relationships with staff who report to them. Bosses who ask their employees to work overtime can try to motivate them with a little talk to lessen their status difference.

The balance between functional conversation and small talk in the workplace depends on the context. And also, it is influenced by the relative power of the two speakers. Usually, the superior defines the conversation because he can close the small talk and "get down to business."

Why small talk matters?

Although talking about the weather or the past weekend may seem unhelpful, knowing how to give this type of conversation is very practical. Small talk is important because it is the beginning of an exchange that can go to more exciting places, it can lead you to meet new people and, above all, you will fall better than if you stay in a corner with the mobile.

Do you expect your date to tell you that they don't want to see you again because you're a petty talker? Few possibilities. You also screw her/him up at a job interview and lose the position you've fought so hard for. Do you expect your potential employers to tell you that you don't know how to get and keep attention? Again, little chance.

It is what makes the prospect of improving your social skills difficult. No one may tell you about your social weaknesses or worse. You may not even realize it until it is too late. It is like a small advantage that can give you abundant benefits in life if you know how to use it wisely. It seems like a slight advantage, but the difference in results between people who lack social skills and those with highly evolved social skills can be staggering.

Social skills can acquire with small talk, constant effort, and mastery of essential techniques. It's not hard to go from being socially awkward to being a social ninja in a few weeks if you use the right advice, make an effort to be socially friendly, and practice without flinching. Therefore, to improve your social skill in small talk, you must first know how to start a conversation. Consequently, we will see below some conversation starters.

Conversation Starters

Sitting down to talk about alcohol, drug, and gambling problems can be scary. Try to use the daily opportunities to speak. They can be in the car, during a meal, or while watching television. Having small talks takes the pressure off a long discussion. Below, we will give you 10 conversation starters.

The next time you want to meet someone, consider using some of the 10 conversation starters. Not only will you feel much more comfortable reaching out to someone, but you will also feel confident because you know what you want to ask or discuss right from the start.

Conversation starters for different scenarios

The 10 conversation starters are great to use to meet new people. While not all of these suggestions are appropriate for all settings, the chances are good that you will find one that fits the different places where you meet other singles.

1. Congratulate the person

Find something that surprises you about the person and start talking to that. If you like what the person is wearing, say, "I noticed how nice your sweater is and wanted to come to say hi to you." You know you are safe with this statement because the person probably would not have worn the sweater if they did not think it was attractive. Be careful with physical attributes, as the person may not have the same thoughts as you about his/

her appearance and may not be comfortable knowing someone noticed, even if you are trying to pay a compliment.

2. Comment on your surroundings

Since you are both in the same environment, you know you are interested in what you are doing. For example, if you are in a museum, you can start the conversation by saying, "I love how this painting reflects the artist's distress over the loss." "What do you think about that?" Even if the person disagrees with what you think, it's a great way to start learning how the person thinks and feels about art. From here, you can go on and discuss other exhibitions. For different settings, pick something to share your thoughts with, and then move on with what he or she thinks.

3. Find a way to help

Suppose you see someone struggling or in need, you can step in to try to help. For example, if you see someone you want to have a conversation with and need help with shopping bags, offer a hand or open a door. If you're in a bar and see that the person is finishing a drink, offer to buy another. These gestures show the person that you are observant and sensitive to the person's needs and wants, which will intrigue him/her. Once you help, you can continue using another of the 10 conversation starters.

4. Ask for help

Many people love to help others in need. It makes them feel unique and worthy. If you are working on a project, ask the person to bring you some material, add something, or contribute to their opinion. Then you can start talking about what you are doing and thanking the person for the help he/she gives you.

5. Participate in the activity

If you are at a club or banquet where there is dancing, approach someone with a smile, and ask him/her to dance. It is a traditional way to meet someone new because having fun with someone makes both of you feel comfortable, making conversation more straightforward. You can talk about how much you like the song, the dance, or whatever else you are enjoying the place.

6. Ask a friend to start the conversation for you

Let a friend start an exchange for you, so you don't have to. If you want to meet someone who knows one of your friends, ask them to introduce you. Ask your friend to think of one thing you and the person have in common and bring this up during the introduction. Your friend will pique the person's interest in question by mentioning a standard part, and then it's your turn to enter the arena.

7. Make a plan

If you are part of a sports team and want to get to know someone on your team or the opposing team better, ask him/her if you would like to meet up to practice. Since you know that the person shares a passion for the same activity, you know that he/she will probably be willing to do it. You can also use this tip if you are at school, asking if he/she wants to study. If it's someone at work, you can ask the person to support you or collaborate with you on a particular project after work at a restaurant or coffee shop.

8. Ask what the person is interested in.

Ask a co-worker or friend what the person you want to meet likes, and then start the conversation on that topic. You can even go one step further by finding a book on the subject, reading it, and then asking if the person has read it. If they have already read it, they can talk about the book, if not, it will be a good recommendation, and you can tell him about it.

9. Bring up something important to you

If you have children or pets, mention them to the person. People who have children or pets are often passionate about them and like to talk about them. Not only will this start a great discussion, but it will also help you learn more about the person.

10. Take an interest in the person

Most people like to talk about themselves. One of the easiest ways to start a conversation is to ask the person what they are like and what interests them.

After using the 10 conversation starters we just saw, you can also start it with a question set. But you should know what those questions are. Therefore, below we are going to give you some of them.

Small Talk Questions

These selections of Small Talk Questions will help you break the ice when you don't know what to talk about with someone you just met or is not very talkative.

1. What's your favorite way to hang out?

Even if it is just doing nothing, we all have an activity with which we like to kill time. It may be one of your first questions to ask someone you know little about.

2. What is the last song you listened to?

This simple question can give us a clue about the other person's musical tastes and can be used as a conversation starter about favorite bands and music.

3. What do you do best?

We all have a skill that stands out above the rest, whether it is profitable or not. Find out which one is yours.

4. What do you do, or what do you study?

The classic "study or work" with which we can start a conversation about studies, jobs, and personal projects.

5. What three words describe you best?

A self-description can tell us a lot about what the person is like and help us get a more in-depth topic of conversation about each one.

6. What is your favorite series?

Nowadays, series are very fashionable, so this is an excellent question to talk with someone, whether they are friends or strangers.

7. Do you like to read?

Another question that allows us to start a conversation is about tastes when it comes to reading. If he/she likes to read, you can keep talking about books.

8. What is your worst hobby?

To a lesser or greater extent, we all have our little hobbies. Find out which one is his/her.

9. And what do you have a mania for?

It is another interesting question to know what can bother that person. Try not to do it in front of her if you want to like her!

10. What is your most absurd fear?

And we all have fears too. Some are very realistic, and then some don't make any sense and are unlikely.

11. If you had to change your name, what other would you choose?

A fun and interesting question to talk with another person, suitable for both friends and people we just met.

12. Where did you spend your last vacation?

This other question tells us if the person likes to travel, but you can also talk about more beach, mountain, or city.

13. What is your best childhood memory?

Childhood anecdotes are always a good icebreaker when we don't know what to talk about.

14. What cartoons did you like as a child?

As children, we have all spent hours in front of the television with our favorite cartoons, and we could spend hours talking about them.

15. What is the app that you use the most on your mobile?

Today most people spend hours in front of their smartphones. Where do they waste the most time?

16. Could you live without a mobile phone?

Another interesting question is to inquire about how much living hooked on the mobile affects us.

17. What country would you like to visit?

This one is the classic question to ask someone looking forward to a trip. It allows you to talk about travel and other cultures.

18. What is your greatest ambition?

Whether big or small, we all have plans and goals that we would like to achieve.

19. If you wrote a book, what would it be about?

It is not so much a question to talk about books, but instead, it tells us a lot about what the other person is like.

20. What is the best advice you have ever been given?

We have all received some advice throughout our lives, some better and some worse. Which one would you share?

21. Who is the person you most admire?

It can be a friend, a family member, a teacher, or your great idol. It is about talking about the values that a particular person transmits to you.

22. What do you think is the best invention ever made?

This question can lead to interesting conversations about the advancements of society and the needs of human beings.

23. If you could travel back in time, what time would you like to visit?

And this curious question allows us to know a little more about the other person.

24. What food could you always eat without getting tired?

It seems like a simple question, but it allows us to open the range of conversations about each one's food and personal tastes.

25. What things reassure you the most?

Another question for when you don't know what to talk about can calm the person or help them relax.

26. Do you have good friends?

With this question, we can know what the social life of the person with whom we are talking is like, and it allows us to raise the issue of what he values in other people.

27. What has been your most significant influence?

There may be a person in our life who has influenced us and made us who we are. But it could also be a book or a movie.

28. What do you think about the current political landscape?

Not everyone likes to chat about politics, but current affairs can be an exciting topic to discuss and break the ice with.

29. What has been your worst experience?

Bad experiences are an exciting topic that we can talk about with another person, and from which we can learn a lot.

How to Talk to Strangers

As we saw above, starting conversations with strangers can be very challenging and stressful for many. Whether at a networking event, at work, or only in the day to day, you should note these 5 tips so that those first talks are not a burden, and you do not feel uncomfortable.

1. Dare to speak

Take off your grief and start a conversation with the person next to you to break the ice. The first word is always the most difficult, but then you will achieve empathy.

2. Ask questions

And it does not mean that you talk about the weather. It implies that you get to know people by asking and asking.

Also, avoid dichotomous questions: those that only have a yes or no answer.

"People are an open book."

3. Pimp the person

It will help you build empathy with others.

People don't remember what you say to them; remember how you make them feel."

4. Watch her

Eye contact is significant in making a good impression, so while you're chatting, look into their eyes and pay close attention.

5. Be present in the conversation

Stop checking your cell phone and focus on listening to everything the other person says.

Now, the answer is the following: what can you do to end a conversation without looking like jerks? Below, let's see 4 ways to do so.

How to end a conversation

When you try to end a person-to-person conversation, you can take more concrete actions, like grabbing your things and saying that you should go, that you are tired or in a hurry, say goodbye, and that's it.

But there are other, more exciting steps to end a conversation. Let's see.

Ending a conversation isn't difficult, but it can feel that way. When it comes time to complete a conversation, it may seem rude or uncomfortable, but it doesn't have to be. Let's see the steps below to do so.

Step #1: Positive conclusion

Always try to end a conversation on a positive note. For example, if you are on the phone and have received monosyllabic responses, just say, "It was great to chat. Can you call back later?" That not only puts the ball in your friend's court, but it also gives them a gracious exit from the conversation.

Step #2: Revive or terminate

What if you've run out of things to say, or if you feel like that's what happened? You then end your current conversation topic and use the question and answer method to resume the conversation. By asking the questions now, you are handing over the reins of the conversation to someone else. By doing so, you can end the conversation entirely.

Step #3: End not so subtle

If you want the conversation to end, a simple, "I have to go. Thanks for chatting with me," cannot be misinterpreted as an attempt to change the subject. Leave no doubt about your desire or need to end the conversation, but end on a positive note.

Step #4: The final hug

If you are talking to someone close to you and having a conversation in person, "Come to that hug," followed by a warm hug, can be an excellent conclusion to the discussion. While in the hug, you can say something like, "It was great to see you today!" or "We must repeat this soon!" It will also indicate the conclusion of the conversation.

Step #5: Making plans

"When can we do this again?" it's a great way to wrap up a face-to-face conversation. "This conversation was excellent; when can we talk again?" works well for text messages or phone conversations too. Don't use this if you never want to talk to this person again because it hints at future interactions.

Step #6: A permanent ending

If your conversation leads to a revelation on your part that you are done with the other person for good, being brash in your conclusion will leave no doubt about your future intentions. "I've said everything I wanted to say, and I have nothing more to say to you. I wish you well, but please don't contact me again" may help a volatile friend or toxic family member understand that the end of the conversation also indicated the end of the relationship.

Step #7: End of emergency

If someone has to leave abruptly due to a real emergency, you can say, "I have to run; this is an emergency. We'll talk later." It is short and to the point, and you are good to go. Don't use this unless it is a real emergency because lying to get off the phone or to get out of a conversation can sometimes come back to bite you later.

How to Get Better at Small Talk

Strategy #1: Practice

The ability to converse is like any other skill. You must practice to master it. If you want to improve, practice having small talk whenever you can.

Tips:

> Choose low-risk situations to practice. If you are going to a party on Friday, you may feel very nervous about chatting with new people, so work on doing it in some less intense social situations. For example, start the small talk in line at the grocery store. Try talking to a server at a coffee shop. If you talk to people that you are unlikely to see again, you may feel calmer.

Strategy #2: Stay positive during small talk

If you feel stressed, you could infect others, so try to develop a positive mindset when you do the converse. If you engage in the situation positively, it will be a more positive experience for everyone. This way, the conversation will be more comfortable, and your social anxiety will calm down in future situations.

Tips:

> Change what you think about small talk. Do not see them as a burden, but as a way to meet new people.

Try doing something to relax, like taking a few deep breaths, before engaging in a situation where you need to talk. You will feel calmer during the problem and will be better equipped to converse positively.

Strategy #3: Listen actively

It is essential that you be a good listener, even during small talk. Active listening is a way to stay focused while talking while showing them that you are paying attention.

Tips:

Use body language to show that you listen. Maintain eye contact, face the person, and nod your head.

Use neutral follow-up phrases to let the person know that you hear them, such as "yeah," "aha," and "I see."

Ask a few questions to keep the person talking or to clarify. When appropriate, you can ask some questions like "What happened next?", "How did you feel?" and "What did you mean when you said__?"

Strategy #4: Read the news

If you have a lot to talk about, small talk will be better. One way to do this is to stay up to date with the news. Most people keep track of current events to some extent. If you can comment on what's going on globally, you'll have great topics for small talk.

Avoid uncomfortable topics. In small talk, some cases should not be touched on as they tend to end conversations and cause discomfort. When engaging in Small Talk, be sure to avoid topics that leave people wondering what to say.

Tips:

- Don't talk too much about yourself. Although you can talk about your own experiences, do not link everything the person says to a personal anecdote.
- Never interrupt. Even if you think you know what the person means, it is considered disrespectful to finish others' sentences.
- Avoid arguing during small talk. If someone brings up a political issue that you disagree with, let it go rather than debate. Some people may take disagreements personally, and you shouldn't risk antagonizing anyone.

Chapter 2. Mastering the Art of Small Talk

In both the introduction and the first chapter, you have seen that small talk is an essential part of socializing and meeting new people. However, it's not always easy to be charming and stay calm during a conversation, especially if you're talking to someone you don't know very well.

However, if you want to improve your small talk skills, you will need a little dedication. First, you must work to decrease anxiety in social settings. You can practice conversations ahead of time to lessen your nerves. Prepare lots of questions to keep the conversation going. You can also bring up some things like the news.

For this reason, in this chapter, I will show you how to develop your social skills in general. Also, I will help you to dare to do something small every day to improve those skills.

The Art of Small Talk and Why It's Worth Your Time

Small talk is often the essential starting point that precedes the more critical conversations that will follow. It is the appetizer that precedes the main course (important conversation).

We could call these more vital conversations, effective conversations. They are the talks that help us achieve our conversational goals. It often requires consideration, reasoning, respect, and diplomacy. A dialogue is needed, a conversation back and forth with one or more people. Patience and excellent listening skills are required. All of this explains why so many of us stick to small talk and rarely move toward useful conversation.

However, a useful conversation is a key to achieving everything you consider essential, both in your professional and personal life. It opens doors for you to develop the skill that will allow you to do what you want and be whom you want to be in this world.

Therefore, it is imperative that you learn the proper techniques to move from small talk to a useful conversation. The skills for both small talk and effective conversations will help you achieve your professional and personal goals.

Best Practices to Improve Your Conversational Skills

1. Start with the best

Don't be picky. If you don't know how to start a conversation, start getting the ball rolling with something easy. If you find it difficult to talk, the best thing is not to begin by analyzing the works of Paul Auster. Relax and ask a simple question.

If you speak to a close person, you can ask something like: "What is the best thing that happened to you today?" In this way, your interlocutor will be remembering positive things and will feel comfortable talking to you. Take as a reference, in the previous chapter, some questions you can make.

If the person you are talking to is unknown, you can turn to a banal theme, such as decorating the place around you or the excellent weather. Or perhaps, telling him/her that you are very excited about something good has happened to you. Making him/her participate in your life (even superficially) will make him/her feel closer to you and more open to conversation.

Above all, don't be dogmatic. Start easy and let the conversation flow. Be flexible and let yourself go.

2. Project into the future

Keep the conversation going by avoiding negativity. The important thing is to focus on the positive, on future things that could go well. For example, tell your boss - the ones who bought the house - how happy they will be in their new home or highlight the advantages of living in a development with a pool.

Take advantage of this section to pay compliments and discover new perspectives, which you may not have known, or offer exciting ideas. In this way, you will be hooking your listener to continue with the conversation.

3. Donot be an expert

Between providing information and being an expert, there is a significant difference. Do you understand the nuance? To have a good conversation, you have to assume that you always have something to learn from the other. If you think that you are the most excellent expert in something, it will not take long for you to realize that you are not the one who knows the most about your specialty and that there are people who know many other things.

On this subject, Seth Godin's post says: Everyone is better than you..." at something. And the same happens to the rest. That is, you will be better than the other person in something, and vice versa. Let's take advantage of this reality to get something positive out of every conversation. The key is to go with an open mind, to think that you can always learn something from each discussion until you end up giving your opinion so that the other party can express themselves more freely. You will have time to respond and argue.

4. Try not to be repetitive

Select simple words that are part of your everyday vocabulary (don't give it up) and don't repeat yourself a lot in the same ideas. If you fall for this, you could bore and confuse the person who is listening to you.

5. Pamper your body language

Maintain eye contact; in this way, you will be showing confidence and interest to the speaker.

Allan Pease, in his book 'Body Language,' explains that "you have to make sure you appear approachable, so keep your body language open. It means you should not cross your arms."

Conversation skills don't improve overnight. Like everything, it takes practice, exercise, and talking a lot. Of course, making you listen is worth it.

Chapter 3. Small Talk Topics

Does this situation sound familiar to you? You're talking to someone, and suddenly the conversation turns cold, and you're both talking about inconsequential things or awkward silence because you both can't think of interesting conversation topics to talk about.

If you are looking for engaging conversation topics for a woman or interesting conversation topics for a man, this section will serve you for anyone.

Your location or venue

If you are both from the same city, one of the topics of conversation that will allow you to start a small talk maybe about your location of residence or the city in which you live. This topic will enable you to create a conversation about the activities that can be enjoyed in the town or which places you like the most. You can talk about the last store they opened or the trendy restaurant.

If you are from different cities, you can take the opportunity to become interested in the place where the other person lives and ask what they like most about living there.

Shows, movies, plays, etc.

Party: Parties evoke positive memories; thinking about parties is usually thinking of fun moments with people we love, which suits us as an exciting topic. Also, everyone has done something crazy at a party.

Music: We will always be within our artillery to resort to music. Music means emotions, art, fun, and good memories for many people.

We'd be crazier than an octopus in a garage if we didn't use it as an exciting topic of conversation.

Movies and Series: Talking about movies or series of the moment is another topic of conversation that can go a long way. You don't have to be a movie buff to start a conversation about the last movie you saw in the cinema or to comment on which series of the moment you are following. If you are lovers of the series and are aware of them, you will have a topic for hours of conversation.

Art

I have already proposed to speak about the cinema. If you already know that he/she is a person interested in these topics to talk about, you can continue there. It will not be necessary to cite the list of impressionist painters or styles of architecture... but it will be required to talk about the emotions that particular works have caused us.

Sample questions:

> Has there been a piece of art that has impressed you a lot?
> What emotions do you feel when you see ...?
> What is the most artistic thing we could do together?

Food, restaurants, or cooking

Food in this century is a topic from which many people can be drawn; among vegans, vegetarians, raw vegans, and all kinds of diets, we can talk about many issues.

Sample questions:

> Have you ever been on a diet?
> What is the craziest diet you've ever heard of?

Hobbies

There are loads of hobbies, martial arts, collecting coins, cooking, karaoke, and knowing the other person's hobbies helps you know more about different facets that he/she has. Therefore, it is quite essential.

Sample questions:

> What are your favorite hobbies?

Do you think hobbits had many hobbies?

Professional interests and responsibilities

One of the classic talking points is Professional interests and responsibilities. To start this topic, you can ask what activities a person does as his/her job. So, showing interest in them telling you more about that person.

You can also talk about your's. Talking about what you do and what you are most passionate about in this life. It is an ideal topic to start a dialogue and get to know the other person more.

Sports

Sports are a topic that can also be talked about if you are both fans. You can talk about the sport you practice or about the team you are fans of.

It is always a good topic for conversation. You will know more about his/her tastes, and you are going to allow your interlocutor to know you a little more. It will also let you think about plans to be able to do together.

Sample questions:

> What is the sport that you have practiced the most in your life?
> Why did you like it so much?
> Are you more into risky sports or more relaxed?

The climate

Another interesting topic of conversation to break the ice can arise from the observations of the climate you are in at that moment. Either talking about the sun that is very hot or it is very cloudy, or for the moment of snow that you have just passed. You could also talk about the storm that made transportation difficult in the city.

Seasons: Seasons or even the weather can be interesting topics.

Sample questions:

> What is your favorite season of the year? Why?
> Are you a person more of sun and beach or more of rain and mountains?

Travel

It is a classic. Most of us have traveled or would love to travel. The trip awakens appetites for adventure, awakens anecdotes, and arouses the desire to grab a backpack and run away.

As a general rule, we keep fascinating stories associated with travel or travel wishes, so why not know them?

Sample questions:

> What has been your best trip?
> Do you have an idyllic destination to travel to? Why?
> Would you preferably travel your whole life or stay in one place, but with a job that gives you a lot of money?

Dating

There are dating of many kinds. Romantic, memorable, interesting, fun ...

Every date we have had with a person says something about us and how we were at that moment in our life. Talking about dating on a date can help you improve it, speaking before the date can help you raise it. The options are enormous. So dating is a good talking point.

Sample questions:

> What has been your most absurd/fun date?
> How would your perfect date be?
> From 1 to 10, how would you rate this quote so far? What could we do to improve it?

Fears

Fears often go hand in hand with a significant emotional charge.

Knowing the fears of another person will help you to understand in greater depth how he/she feels and what he/she is like. And therefore, they will simplify the process of connecting with him/her. Very few people usually talk about their fears regularly, so it is also an original topic that will surprise you.

Sample questions:

> What are your biggest fears?
> Have you ever overcome any fear?

Are you afraid of being kisses on the cheek? Well, I'm going to do it.

Childhood

We have all been children, and most of us associate childhood with tenderness, innocence, and positive memories. It is also an epic of our life that links us a lot to others since we have all done similar things when we were little.

Sample questions:

What did you play when you were little?
What is the best memory of your childhood?

Animals

Animals are a conversational classic on a date. If he/she had a pet, we are probably arousing many emotions. Likewise, we can also play with which animal she, you, and how those animals would get along.

Sample questions:

What has been your favorite pet?
If you were an animal, what animal would you be?
What is the most animalistic thing you have done with someone you like?

Literature

Books, poems, essays, stories, literature is one of the world's cultural pillars; the number of possible conversations there are inexhaustible, so enjoy it.

Sample questions:

> What book would you like to write about?
> What was the first book you read that you have evidence of?
> What name would we give a book about ourselves?

You and I

The crux of the matter. The creme de la creme of exciting topics to talk about. The gold medal goes to the one who speaks… about oneself and the other. The binomial that we form in that place at that time.

Here we can extract gold from questions and issues.

Sample questions:

> What things do you and I have in common, after all we've talked about?
> What things do you like about me?

Challenges

Challenges put us to the test and are a way of testing our

willpower, sacrifice, etc. Facing and overcoming challenges says a lot about us and is a beautiful topic of conversation.

Sample questions:

> What is your biggest challenge today?
> What is the challenge that you feel most proud to have overcome?

Chapter 4. Make Successful Small Talk

"A good conversation should exhaust the subject, not the interlocutors." -Winston Churchill

The success of a Small Talk comes into play in the preparation process. It is convenient to consider a series of tips and techniques to ensure what you want to say, duration, and transmission of the message are optimal.

The best news is that all soft skills can significantly improve with the right techniques and practice. We speak of an "art" that is learned through practice. In this section, I will show you how you can get success when making small talk.

The 5 steps to make a successful small talk

Step #1: Listen actively

Knowing how to listen to another is not increasing the number of sounds that the ear can perceive. Good listening is active. That is, participatory.

Listen actively prevents the dialogue from turning into a monologue. When only one of the two is speaking, there is no conversation. Of course, there is always a certain asymmetry. Someone talks more, and someone listens more. It is challenging to achieve an absolute balance, but the closer you get to it, the better the dialogue will be.

Step #2: Rescue the terminal pauses

There is always a moment when silence makes its appearance. Some people are deeply uncomfortable with that. But sometimes, it is not wrong. Pauses are also necessary. However, when the silence lasts too long, and you do not want to end the conversation yet, the right thing is to rescue the dialogue from that void.

How to do it?

The best way is by entering transition phrases. These statements allow the dialogue to be hooked up again, taking it to a previous topic or a new topic. They are expressions such as "About what you were saying before …", "Changing the subject, I would like to know what you think of …" "I had not told you that …" These are phrases that help you chain and help maintain a good conversation.

Step #3: Release information

Releasing information has to do with answering our interlocutor's questions with quality content. If you answer laconically or limit yourself to monosyllables, you will frustrate the other's will to nurture and maintain successful small talk.

By answering the other's questions giving additional information, you will facilitate the dialogue. It is also a sign of openness and desire to make known what you think, feel, or believe. It makes interaction easier. You have to give an extensive answer, but you have to provide additional information to those requested.

Step #4: Self-disclosure

Human beings are more likely to give our trust to people who also provide it to us. So, we tend to be more open with those who adopt the same attitude. If you want a conversation to move towards a more personal level, it is advisable that you start by sharing content at this level. Reveal to the other aspects that have to do with the private sphere of your life.

Thus, if you speak spontaneously about these personal aspects, the other person is likely to be motivated to do so as well. All of this leads to a move from a polite and formal conversation to a more personal one.

Step #5: Questions

In the previous chapters, we have seen, on several occasions, that the question is the key to make great small talk. Questions help move the conversation forward. Not only do they allow you to explore and get to know each other better, but they also turn out to be an indispensable condiment for maintaining a good conversation. You have to have enough criteria to choose the questions to be asked of the other. The goal is not to make you feel questioned or invaded.

If you do not know a person well, it is best to ask questions that go from the most superficial to the parts that may be more compromising. In this way, you will allow time for confidence to increase naturally, and you will not generate moments of discomfort.

No doubt cultivating the art of good conversation pays off. Not only does it get you into entertaining situations, but it is also therapeutic. It allows you to express yourself, listen, and learn from others. It also enriches your life and gives more color to your relationships with others.

Practice #1: Small talk at a rail station

These are two unknowns. But person A is always afraid when he/she has to ask a stranger (Person B) something. Now, it is time to ask about a destination at a train station. How will he do it?

> A: Good morning, are there roundtrip tickets?
> B: No, the single ticket of ten trips is used for the metro and bus.
> A: Do you know how much does it cost?
> B: 5.20 Euros.
> A: Do you know how to go to Avenida de America station, please?
> B: You have to take line 2, the red one, in the direction of Fourth Way, and get off at Canal. There you change and take line 7, the orange, towards The Corner and get off at 1,2,3: the third station.
> A: Wow! You are a great person. My name is (....). What is yours?
> B: (The name)

A: You know! I always traveled by train. But, for the first time, I have taken that way. But sorry for the inconvenience.

B: You don't bother me. Instead, thank you for letting me help you. I like to help.

As you can see, in this small talk, Person A uses only questions. As we have seen previously, the questions are fundamental until the two became confident to speak more openly. There is no doubt that this conversation can go further if either of them wants it to.

Practice #2: Small talk at the Office

Jhon is very shy. Although he falls in love with Margaret, he is not very open with the company's other colleagues. Luckily, Margaret left her Office and gone to her friends, near Jhon's Office, and forgot her umbrella. Jhon noticed but stepped forward to take advantage of the circumstance. How will he do it?

Jhon: Whose umbrella is this?
Mary: I don't know, it's not mine.
Jhon: Did someone forget an umbrella in the hallway?
Albert: Not me.
Donnie: Not me.
John: So, who left it?
Mary: Margaret was here earlier. It's probably hers.
John: I'm going to call her to let her know that it's here.

First, it is necessary to point out that a dialogue presents an initial intention to communicate something on the part of a character, which can be reduced to a greeting or a call for attention from one person to another to start the conversation. That's what Jhon does.

Jhon already gave the obligation to himself to call Margaret so that she would find out about the loss of her umbrella. There is no doubt that Jhon is eager to deliver that news that Margaret wants to hear so much. It is a good start for Jhon to have a good relationship with Margaret.

Practice #3: Small talk at a Party

Jimmy is in love with Dany's sister while Jimmy never talks to Dany as he shows his disagreement with the relationship. But, one of the students at the school threw a party. Dany and her sister were invited. How will Jimmy take advantage of that moment to talk to Dany?

> Jimmy: Hello, Dany, how are you?
> Dany: good, and how have you been throughout the party:
> Jimmy: Great! Can I ask you something?
> Dany: Of course!
> Jimmy: Why did your sister not come to the party?
> Dany: Because she is sick
> Jimmy: and what does she have?
> Dany: She is throwing up.
> Jimmy: Wow! that hurts to hear it. OK, thank you very much for letting me know. I will do my best to visit her

after the party. In the meantime, if you arrive first, say hello to me.

Sometimes the interest we have in getting something motivates us to start a small talk. Therefore, it is always good to keep in mind why you should create a conversation. As we have seen previously, small talk is the door to successful conversations.

So, keep in mind that reason to motivate yourself to start your small talk soon.

Small Talk Quiz

The objective of this Small Talk Quiz is to help you capture the interlocutor's attention to be sure. So, you can start a conversation with him/her.

Of course, they are just examples to inspire you and look for the ones that best suit your way of being and the situation.

Instead of asking	Try
How are you?	What's your story?
How was your day?	What did you do today?
Where are you from?	What is the most exciting thing that happened at work today?
What do you do?	How did you get into that line of work?
What line of work are you in?	What is the meaning of your name? What would you like it to mean?

What's your name?	What do you want to do this weekend?
How was your weekend?	Who do you think is the luckiest person in this room?
Would you like to have some...?	What memories does this house bring you?
How long have you been living here?	If you could teleport right now, where would you go?

From commitment talk to interest in the other

If also you want this conversation to be meaningful, you can try using one of the following ten questions:

1. What are you most passionate about right now?
2. If irrefutable proofs of God's existence appeared today, what would you do? What if there was irrefutable evidence to the contrary?
3. What is the most important thing I should know about you?
4. If you died today, how do you think you would be remembered? Would you regret anything?
5. What is your biggest fear?
6. If you could go back in time, what advice would you give yourself?
7. Do you think that emotions are useful?
8. What is the name of your oldest friend? How did you meet?
9. What do you miss about your childhood?
10. What makes you smile just thinking about it?

Example of how to break the mirror

When you meet strangers, try to be polite and repeat the observations they make. This attitude is known as the mirror phenomenon.

For example:

> Dave: Today is a beautiful day!
> Patty: Yes, it is a beautiful day!

By repeating people's opinions and language, you eliminate the possibility of deepening the conversation.

Instead…, do this

> Dave: Today is a beautiful day!
> Patty: It's perfect for going to the beach!

Patty avoided falling into the boring yes/no conversation and instead shared her taste for the beach and even motivated the conversation.

Give an unexpected answer

To avoid falling into the mirror phenomenon, you can use an unexpected answer.

instead of

Dave: How was your trip?

Robert: My trip was good!

Carly: It's very hot today

Curtis: Yes, it is very hot.

Try

Dave: How was your trip?

Robert: The prices of the airlines are crazy. I don't know if they charge by weight or by CI.

Carly: It's very hot today

Curtis: In this dimension, yes.

These are just a few ideas you can use to start a great conversation and open yourself up to the possibilities of meeting new people.

Chapter 5. How To Make Effortless Small Talk

Starting a conversation with a stranger can create much anxiety.

We are social, even if you insist otherwise

Do you remember when you were a kid? It was all a game, and if something made you nervous, you used to interpret it as emotion, not fear. It was probably easy for you to go to the new neighbor's house to ask if you could come in to meet his/her son.

What has changed so that we now isolate ourselves and suffer from anxiety in social gatherings? Well, the passing of the years has shown us the bitter face of society. Having been rejected several times, we have learned not to expose ourselves so cheerfully.

That has caused, according to a study[1], we incorrectly assume that strangers do not want to talk to us. Do you remember the "Don't talk to strangers" that your mother used to repeat to you? The moral is that we assume, incorrectly, that people do not

---

1   Jonathan Gerber, Ladd Wheeler, May 5, 2017. On Being Rejected: A Meta-Analysis of Experimental Research on Rejection. Retrieved from: https://doi.org/10.1111/j.1745-6924.2009.01158.x

want to talk to us. And since the stranger sitting next to us also believes it, the result is that no one takes the first step.

People tend to wait for him to reveal the magic phrase that will allow them to start a dialogue with anyone and in any situation.

The problem is that the phrase itself is given too much importance when it has none. Of course, the attitude with which you say is much more critical. And not even that: the mere act of reaching out and opening your mouth is more than many others do.

10 practical strategies to make effortless small talk

1. Get rid of embarrassment with the Mask technique

The Mask Technique consists of creating an alter ego, a character that allows you to leave your everyday reality to do and say things that you would not normally do. This way, if someone rejects you, you can be sure that they reject your character.

This technique is used by actors and comedians like Daniel Tosh to overcome his shyness on stage. Even Beyoncé has created an alter ego named Sasha for when she has to act. You can click here to read the article on Showbiz CheatSheet. In both cases, extroverted and provocative characters have been invented, and when it corresponds, they act as such.

Logically, in the long run, it is much better to overcome shyness by facing its origin, but the Mask technique is a handy tool to start behaving in a more relaxed and sociable way.

2. Never forget your real goal

It is the main reason many people fail before they even try.

When you want to start a dialogue with someone, you must be clear that your goal is not to impress, try to be liked, or appear an exciting person. People don't know. Any of these three attempts can easily interpret against you.

- Your goal should only be to show yourself as sociable and calm, who wants to have a conversation to see if there are common ground.
- Then you can set more specific secondary objectives, such as exchanging business cards or giving each other the phone to meet another time, but for now, you should not think of any more.

The moment you are clear that your goal is to find common interests to turn them into conversations, you will stop being distracted by other matters that get you out of your way.

3. Smile, and the world will smile at you

Before articulating the first word, this simple gesture can differentiate between a good or bad first impression.

By now, we are all aware of the power of smiling. Several articles show that the simple act of nodding and smiling when you come across a stranger on the street can create a connection. Not to mention the entire collection of research showing that smiling increases your attractiveness.

It does not mean that you permanently force a grimace of joy on your face. It would not be honest, and it would look very unnatural. More than just smiling, it's about your attitude.

When you start a conversation for the first time with someone, you should do it with a positive and friendly attitude.

Show that you come to provide energy, not to suck it up. Nobody wants to put up with ash for half an hour, so from the outset, you have to predispose people so that they don't see you like that kind of person. Smile, and others will smile back.

Below you will find examples of phrases that can be very strange without the correct intonation and non-verbal language. So, the essential point on this list is, without a doubt, this.

4. Prepare the ground with this simple phrase

"How is the day going?" "Hi! How are you?" "Hi, how's everything?"

I could put many more variants, but the objective is that your interlocutor answers that it is OK. These types of questions are especially interesting because it has been shown in a study[2] that by answering "well," your interlocutor will be more predisposed to have a social behavior.

When someone tells you that they are fair or perfect, they will hardly behave negatively immediately afterward. So, the right idea is that your first sentence is a simple "Hello, how are you?"

If the other person is doing something or just for education, it is also best to start asking for permission with an "Ex-

---

2   Daniel J. Howard: The Influence of Verbal Responses to Common Greetings on Compliance Behavior: The Foot-In-The-Mouth Effect. Retrieved from: https://doi.org/10.1111/j.1559-1816.1990.tb00399.x

cuse me" or "Sorry." Especially when you want to enter the conversation of a group since it shows education and that you are aware of others' social situations.

Asking if you can interrupt him/her for a second is another excellent idea because this study showed that it improves your interlocutor's predisposition to talk to you by trying to be consistent with his/her answer.

5. Ask something related to the situation or place

The most natural way to start a conversation is to make a comment or question about the situation you and the other person share. Not because of its simplicity it is less effective, and, after all, it is the only bond you have before meeting.

This way of initiating conversations also prevents shy people from being rejected if it happens, as they can always justify that they just wanted to ask something.

According to Dr. Carducci, director of the Shyness Research Institute, the initial question does not have to be incredibly creative: the best phrase is simple and should only refer to the shared environment or situation. Ideally, an open question so that you cannot be answered with just a yes or no. Here are some examples:

In a bar: "Excuse me, do you know what time this place closes?"
In a training course: "In which classroom is the next lecture?"
At the station: "Do you know when the last train leaves?"

Even if you think a question may be too obvious, don't worry. These phrases can interpret as that you really need the information or just want to start a conversation. Hence it doesn't matter much what you say.

6. Show curiosity about what you are doing

This strategy is not the most appropriate if the other is not doing anything special, such as waiting at a bus station, but it can be useful in gyms, social clubs, or bars.

You also expose yourself very little since you only show yourself as a curious person. It is a very safe way to start a conversation as long as your attitude is positive and judgmental.

In a gym, you could ask someone who was exercising something like, "Excuse me, what muscles do you strengthen with that exercise?" On a soccer field, you could ask the person next to you if what is blowing is a vuvuzela. Even in A restaurant, you could ask the customer near your table what they ordered, with the excuse that it looks good.

7. Compliment and continue with a question

This option is beneficial when the person you want to talk to is not doing anything particularly interesting, nor is the situation binding you in any way.

It consists of starting with a genuine compliment that predisposes the other person to be friendly with you (liking generates liking) and then following up with a question that leads to the conversation.

Some formulas that have given me excellent results are evaluating someone's dress, shoes, or mobile phone, such as:

> "You match that tie well with your suit. Where did you buy it?"
>
> "I like your hat; do you sell it in Barcelona?"

8. Ask for a recommendation, advice, or opinion

It is similar to the previous one, but with nuances. For starters, several studies have shown that asking someone for their opinion is tremendously helpful in making an excellent first impression. Everyone likes to feel valued, and one of the easiest ways to do this is by asking for a recommendation.

When you ask someone for advice, you are implicitly showing that you value their judgment, and that's flattering. Logically, if you don't know the person, your interest shouldn't be too deep.

> "Sorry, what phone is that? I am thinking of buying a new one. "
>
> "Excuse me. I saw that you are reading the latest Murakami book. Would you recommend it to me? "
>
> "Hello, if you come here often, would you mind pointing me to a dish that was good?"

The idea is that you take advantage of the situation and context of the person you want to talk to ask for a recommendation, and from there, you develop a conversation.

9. Fill in the information gaps

So far, we've seen pretty roundabout ways to start a conversation, but the best of all is explicit honesty.

Being explicitly honest is nothing more than filling in the information gaps. It is achieved by giving a what, a why, and a when. The reason is that many times the information we provide is not complete, which causes our interlocutors to end up filling it in with their imagination. And that doesn't always work in our favor.

See the difference:

> Hello, what is your name?

Here you do not give any information, and your interlocutor can imagine what he wants. Perhaps he thinks that you want to connect with him/her, or that you have recognized him/her, but you do not remember your name, or that you want to attract his / her attention for some reason. You do not control what your interlocutor will think of you.

> Hi, I'm trying to meet new people instead of talking to the same older adults. Do you mind if I introduce myself, and that is how we meet?

In this case, you clearly say what you want (to introduce yourself), why you want it (because you always talk to them) and what you want it for (to meet new people). You do not allow any wrong interpretation.

Being honest with what you want and making it evident upfront is probably the most natural way to start a conversation with strangers. It takes practice, but once mastered, the chances of rejection are meager.

10. Give a way out and avoid rejection

Finally, another way to reduce the other person's chances of telling you that talking is not going well right now is to provide an easy way out.

People often get defensive when a stranger approaches them because they are not sure if it will be too heavy, and they fear that they will not be able to shake it off for a long time.

To prevent your interlocutor from being invaded by this thought, give him/her the exit yourself. It means that at the beginning of the conversation, you mention that you can only speak for a short period because they are waiting for you elsewhere. You free him/her from the feeling of being trapped with you. You provide both of you with a comfortable outlet in case things don't go well.

Also, when people think you have to leave soon, they relax. If you walk up to someone in a bar and say, "Hi, I'd like to meet you," their defenses kick in. Who are you? What do you want? So, when do you leave? Filling in the information gaps, you answer the first two, but you must also answer the last one.

> Hello, I am expecting some friends, and since you also seem to be waiting, I wondered if I can sit with you for 5 minutes until they come. Do you mind?

If the conversation goes well, don't worry that no one will remember the 5 minutes you mentioned at the beginning.

Chapter 6. Overcoming Shyness And Fear

Some people have more difficulties and mental barriers in speaking or relating to others. Shyness is a personality trait often accompanied by fears and insecurities; a shy person often enjoys their own company and immerses themselves in their inner world to feel more comfortable. However, on some occasions, the fact that it is difficult for us to establish social connections or speak in public can become a problem that must be solved immediately. So, it is essential to learn the best strategies to know how to overcome shyness and insecurity.

Being shy is not something categorically wrong. But it can generate adaptation and relationship difficulties if social skills are not worked on. You can put your efforts to adapt better and lead a life far from the fear that social relationships can cause you.

Why Is Confidence Important?

Simply put, self-confidence is trusting in your abilities.

It is very different from being overconfident or having an ego. Having false confidence can cause many problems. Having an ego can cause many problems.

But, when you have genuine confidence and believe in yourself, no task or goal seems insurmountable. Even if you are faced with something you don't know how to do, you have enough faith in yourself to learn how to do it. Similarly, even if you are faced with a difficult decision, self-confidence means that you are confident in your ability to choose the best path for yourself.

Confidence is essential for many reasons. First of all, when you have confidence in yourself, it means that you believe in yourself. You have full faith in your skills and decision-making abilities.

Even if you don't know how to do something or achieve something, confidence gives you the boost you need to find the answers.

Other people also notice confidence. They are typically leaders in their families, their communities, and in their workplaces. People are attracted to them and are more likely to listen to and respect them.

Focus on the Present Know Thyself

"Know Thyself," then, is the obligation of each individual: understand, accept, study your soul, which is the real object of knowledge of a person, because only in this way can you guide your own life and actions according to your purposes and interests.

This phrase considers self-knowledge as a fundamental step to access knowledge, to the truth of things, to reach in wisdom the level of the divine, the prophetic, and the oracular.

"Know Thyself!" it also has the appeal of self-help. Is your goal to accept yourself? Well, you need to get to know yourself first. Or is it making good decisions, the decisions that are right for you? Again, this would be not easy unless you know yourself. This whole "Knowing Thyself" is not as simple as it sounds. It could be a severe philosophical mess, not to mention lousy advice.

To be honest with yourself, you need to be aware and know yourself well. Knowing yourself encompasses everything from naming your favorite color to acknowledging your failures and weaknesses and accepting them for what they are. Being authentic is more than memorizing a list of strengths and weaknesses for a job interview. It can talk openly about how you failed in that job interview without resorting to denial or blaming someone else. It is to recognize that you need help to achieve your goal of quitting smoking.

Self-awareness is the understanding of your weaknesses and strengths to assess and reevaluate who you are today, whom you want to be tomorrow, and the challenges that will be unique to you along the way.

What Is in Keeping with Your Character?

To define character, you should know that character develops over the years and living with your environment. In other words, you are not born with it, nor is it a genetic trait.

Character is a set of positive characteristics that we all have and that we refine over time. These characteristics are closely linked to your convictions, beliefs, and values. When you have established each of these, your character will be the one that will defend your point of view.

As time passes, you focus and prioritize your activities based on your convictions and values, and your character will form more and more.

Something that could happen to you is that you think that character and temperament are the same, but they are not. Temperament is a trait that has been proven to be inherited and genetic.

How to have an attractive character in your relationships?

Think of a person you admire a lot, whom you consider is determined in the things he/she does and who has magnetic relationships in his/her life. You already did? The safest thing is that this someone has a defined character that is continually developing.

So how to have an attractive character knowing the above and its meaning?

Do your best to define what you believe in and your guiding values in your life. The great ones do it, and you must do it too. If you can do it, people will know more clearly who you are. It will let them know what to expect from you and build trust, which will cause them to interact much more with you.

When this happens, your life will flow much more, your relationships will be more sincere, and in the business field, if you like them, you will form more emotional commercial ties guided by trust.

Building a person's character is a robust process that we all go through at some point in our lives. It can make you become someone with a high magnetism that attracts relationships and good things to your life.

If you don't think so, believe the great leaders who have made changes in society. These have been beings with a highly developed character, which has made it easier for them to realize their dreams.

5 tips to improve the character

Tip 1: Keep exposing yourself to situations where your emotions get upset. Continue to train your state of consciousness and know when you want to tell your ideas.

Tip 2: Think and reflect. What upsets you? Why do you want to have a character? Do you have any pent-up emotions? Finding these, you can draw a strategy.

Tip 3: Determine your convictions, beliefs, and values. Do you already know who you are and what you stand for? Being aware of this gives you confidence in yourself and builds confidence in others by knowing what to expect from you.

Tip 4: Communicate only when necessary. If you know who you are, you don't seek approval from others, and you won't find yourself in the exhausting process of speaking what you would like others to hear from you. Perhaps this is the best way to know how to have character. When you have it, you will become a magnet, and people will be the ones who will ask your opinion. That is, they will try to communicate with you and not the other way around.

Tip 5: Read and listen to audios on personal development. If people knew how powerful these tools are, the world would be much better than it already is. Many authors have experienced a lack of character in their lives and are happy to share with you how they managed to raise it to a level of success.

And you? Do you know how to have a character, or do you already consider that you have it?

And are you a shy person, and are you looking for strategies to break this barrier that prevents you from relating to others? Discover the best steps, tips, and exercise below.

4 main steps to overcome shyness and fears

Step #1: Know your strengths and weaknesses

To overcome shyness and fears, it is essential to do a personal self-knowledge exercise to identify what you must improve and what are your best tools. Knowing your weaknesses does not make you more vulnerable. On the contrary, you can know what attitudes you will have to change and to overcome shyness thanks to this exercise.

Step #2: Trust yourself and don't compare yourself

Many times, shyness arises from the fear of feeling inferior to others. You may not speak for fear of saying something wrong or uncomfortable. Trust yourself. You sure have a lot to contribute to the conversation. Nor is it very appropriate to compare yourself with other people. Each individual has their way of behaving and relating to others. An extroverted person may find it easier to start a conversation. However, this fact does not mean that they are a better person than someone introvert.

Step #3: Pursue small goals

For such a significant behavior change, it's a good idea to set realistic, short-term goals. Taking small steps will raise your self-esteem, and you will see that. Indeed, you can get out of your bubble of shyness and introversion. You can try going to social gatherings with a small number of people, trying to start a conversation with an acquaintance, going to a friend's party ...

Step #4: Psychological therapy

Fortunately, there are many treatments to overcome shyness and fear of speaking. Cognitive-behavioral therapy is usually very indicated to cure this problem. They could be on the following points:

    Assessment of the situation

- Search for other psychological problems that interact with fear
- Social skills training
- Practice for starting and holding conversations
- Facing criticism
- Public speaking practice
- Monitoring and evaluation of therapy

Tips and Tricks to Lose Shyness

Along with cognitive-behavioral therapy, we can practice the following tricks at home. These can help us overcome everyday situations that generate fear and insecurity:

- Manage anxiety through relaxation techniques (meditation, breathing, mindfulness).
- Start positive thinking to fight fear.
- Do exercises to strengthen self-esteem and self-confidence.
- Practice your communication skills in front of a mirror.
- In giving a presentation in public, relax a few minutes before and do not obsessively practice the speech.

Exercises to overcome shyness

It is important to remember that shyness is not an inherently negative characteristic. The diversity in personalities makes human beings an incredible and very varied species in terms of their behavior. However, when a personality trait prevents you from leading an everyday life, it is time to treat it. Here are the following exercises to learn how to overcome shyness and insecurity.

Exercise #1: Trust in your abilities to communicate

if even we do not trust and assert ourselves, no one will. Self-esteem and the reinforcement of self-esteem are the first steps to fighting against fear and shyness.

Exercise #2: Admit your personality

Don't force yourself to be someone else. Admit your shyness and work your communication skills through it. Do you want to know how to stop being shy? First of all, you will have to accept yourself and observe your personality tendencies.

Exercise #3: Practice assertive communication

It is based on expressing and defending our emotions without fear but in a calm and non-aggressive way.

Exercise #4: Learn to accept compliments

A shy person has many difficulties accepting compliments and responding to them with a simple "thank you." When someone you trust tells you how well you do something or how handsome you are today, accept what they are saying, allow yourself to believe that someone is telling you something positive. Taking lovely comments from people you trust can help you improve the image you project towards others.

Exercise #5: Try to make a new friendship

Introversion can lead to isolation and, in turn, lead to even more shyness. You can try to overcome shyness by stepping out of your comfort zone and establishing a new personal bond with someone.

Chapter 7. Using Body Language in Small Talk

The communication we make through our body has a significant influence on social relationships and is the perfect mirror of emotions.

It has happened to everyone that they have met a person, but they did not convey confidence. There is a contradiction between what they are communicating verbally and what their body language is saying.

On other occasions, the opposite may happen, that we meet someone who has coordinated body language and verbal communication and gives us good feelings.

Body language is a form of non-verbal communication based on the gestures, postures, and movements of the body and face to transmit information. It is usually done unconsciously, so it is a good indicator of the person's emotional state.

What Exactly Are Nonverbal Cues?

Nonverbal Care capable of delivering telltale messages. Successful interactions depend on both parties being able to use and read body language. Learn how to build confidence at work using proper non-verbal expressions.

From the way you stand to the way you talk to your interlocutor. Her gestures can reveal the level of attention or empathy for the other members of her team. Correct posture, appropriate facial expression, and the right tone of voice are essential if you want to convey confidence in small talk.

To correctly interpret the stimuli you emit and receive, it is necessary to be attentive to facial expressions, movements of arms, legs, hands, head, and chest. The tone of voice, volume, and speed of speech also communicate, as well as appearance says a lot about who we are and how we feel.

Being aware of the signals you send is vital to know the type of information you want to share. To do this, it is also necessary to identify which position is the most suitable for each situation. Studies on body expression have been intensified in recent years by professionals in psychology and sociology to identify feelings and expressions not communicated by words. For this reason, below, I will give you some nonverbal cues and meanings.

Nonverbal cues and its meanings

Eye contact

This factor depends, to a great extent, on the person who receives it, and therefore within non-verbal language, it can have a positive or negative reading. It depends on the feelings that the reaction provoked in the person.

Prolonged eye contact

Looking into a person's eyes for an extended period can mean that you are lying to that person. In this way, he maintains his gaze, sometimes without blinking, to avoid being discovered in the deception.

Look sideways

It is an action that can have a negative meaning since, in non-verbal language, it means boredom and that you are looking for escape routes to distract yourself.

Touch your nose

It is another of the great acquaintances in body language. The primary meaning is that the person making the gesture is lying, but sometimes it can mean that the person is angry or upset.

Shrug your shoulders

It is a universal movement within a non-verbal language, and it means not knowing what is happening. Generally, this shoulder movement is accompanied by open palms, slight hunching of the back, and a raised eyebrow.

Crossed arms

It is a well-known defensive body language stance that signifies rejection or disagreement. But you have to be careful with this gesture because it can mean that the person is cold, so you must take the context into account.

Arms crossed with thumbs up

It has a similar meaning to crossing the arms, but the thumbs-up's position indicates that the person wants to convey pride.

Hands behind your back

It is a position that demonstrates confidence and shows that the person speaking is not afraid. Also, this posture can help you gain confidence in times of insecurity.

Trembling legs

When a person has tremors in their legs, it can mean that they are in anxiety, irritated, or both.

Voice tone and volume

Voice tone and volume are some of the essential elements in the non-verbal language.

As a clarification, we can say that the tone is the voice's timbre, while the volume is the intensity of it.

Thanks to the union of these two elements, within the non-verbal language, we can find several meanings:

- Sadness: It occurs when there are a low volume and a solemn tone in the voice.
- Joy: It occurs when there are a high volume and a harsh tone in the voice.
- Disinterest: It occurs when there are a low volume and tone in the voice.
- Nervousness: It occurs when there is a medium-high volume, and you babble.
- Surprise: It occurs when there is a high pitch, fast speed, and

accentuated pronunciation in the voice.

Confidence: It occurs when there is a high volume, a determined tone, and you speak at a medium speed.

Fake smiles

Another of the great acquaintances of body language is when someone is forcing a smile. A genuine smile is one in which wrinkles appear in the areas near the eyes. For this reason, fake smiles are those that do not have those wrinkles.

Rest your chin on your hands

It is a gesture that within a non-verbal language can have several readings depending on the position of the palm:

Open palm: It can have a meaning of boredom or lack of interest.

Closed palm: It can mean that the person is evaluating what is said or done.

Head high and chin forward

You have heard the phrase "go with your head high" on many occasions. When a person performs this gesture, it is read in non-verbal communication as a sign that expresses aggressiveness and power.

Touch your ear

On many occasions, this gesture means the desire to block or not listen to the words being heard. But if the context is a conversation between two people, it may mean that the person believes that you are hiding something. Touching the ear implies the desire to block out what is being heard

Scratching your neck

When a person makes this gesture while talking to you, they are unsure of what they are saying.

Closed jaw + tight neck + frown

It is a set of gestures that occur when there is a situation with which you are dissatisfied.

Nod your head

It is a contagious gesture, which, in most cases, has a positive meaning since it communicates interest and agreement. When the motion is made several times and at high speed, it means that you no longer want to listen.

Interlace the fingers of the hands

Generally, this position of the hands is negative and conveys an anxious or repressed attitude.

Join fingertips

Although it seems incredible, it has the opposite meaning of intertwining your fingers. In non-verbal language, this position of the hands signifies confidence and security but can sometimes be confused with arrogance.

Understanding Body Language in Context

As I have already mentioned, nonverbal cues and reading

signals play an essential role in our daily communication. This communication is characterized by a person's facial language, gestures, body posture, and movements. The following examples show how even the smallest movements reveal our feelings.

Facial expression

Facial expression encompasses all the movements that can be read on a person's face. One of the most vital signs of facial expression is the smile. It enables open communication with strangers, shows kindness, understanding, and joy, and is the perfect signal to start a conversation.

Emotions are transmitted, to a large extent, through the eyes and mouth, and the features of the face only intensify them. A look can denote interest, absence, affection, hatred, doubt, curiosity, or fear, and we can perceive all this in fractions of a second.

Interest/curiosity: the eyes are awake and open and look calmly at the person speaking or the object being said to absorb all the information in a concentrated way. But beware: if direct eye contact lasts too long, other people quickly find it unpleasant or heavy.

Disinterest: the view travels around the room or surroundings and lingers here and then on other people and other events. A completely off-center, motionless gaze signifies that you have become self-absorbed and is focused on your thoughts.

Surprise: eyes open sharply, and eyebrows move upward.

Anger: Eyes tighten, eyebrows are drawn together, and the

forehead is furrowed.

Doubt: the gaze is concentrated, but the eyes are restless because the listener reflects at the same time if he/she can believe what is being said. Depending on the posture regarding what is being said, the eyebrows may flick in disbelief or gather in irritation.

Fear: the eyes also open sharply with trepidation; simultaneously, the pupils are spread widely to perceive all the possible details of the threat.

If you want to learn how to understand body language correctly, it is best to pay attention to the pupils. They are especially treacherous, as their movements cannot consciously control, and yet they reflect emotions. Thus, the pupils dilate when we feel joy or other positive stimuli and narrow when we feel fear or aversion.

How to Use Body Language When Making Small Talk

There are several functions that non-verbal messages fulfill:
- Emphasize the verbal message (consciously or unconsciously).
- Repeat the verbal message, for example, by waving your hand after saying goodbye.
- Substitute the verbal message; for example, wave your hand to say goodbye.
- Show the necessary attitudes of the receiver and regulate communication. For example, with non-verbal signals,

we show interest, disgust, encourage a change of topic, reinforce the exposition and contradict or distort the verbal message, and, when this occurs, the interlocutor receives the non-verbal message.

To avoid having bad small talk, you must know how to use your Body Language. Let's see how to do so.

Keys to make small talk when using non-verbal cues

1. Make the smile part of the regular repertoire

When initiating small talk and tense situations, the smile is a widely used weapon mainly. When you smile, it is a "mirror effect" in the interlocutor and that, thanks to the sensation of cause-effect, generates positive feelings in both interlocutors.

2. Show expressiveness but not overreact

Keep fingers together when gesturing, hands below chin level, and avoid crossing arms or feet.

3. Use open gestures

For example, show your hands, stretch your arms and legs, spread your shoulders, do not put objects between your own body and the interlocutor, such as tables, folders, or books, and make sure that the face is visible.

4. Use gestures that accompany the speech and facilitate understanding

For example, gesturing a measurement or a distance, pointing to a direction, describing a rhythm, or stretching two fingers of the hand while saying that two key ideas will present.

5. Avoid gestural tics that are sometimes caused by nervousness

Avoid playing with a pen or with the ring, brushing your hair, putting on your glasses...

6. Support the conversation with the movement of the head

Use a triple nod when speaking and head tilt when listening. Keep your chin up.

7. Check eye contact

Practice eye contact but avoid contact when it is aggressive or uncomfortable for others. People who watch are more credible than those who don't.

8. Control body posture in conversations sitting at a table

It is not advisable to lie on it but neither disappear after it sinking into the chair. Lean forward when you listen and stand tall when you speak. Always keep your arms on the table. Avoid closed hands and crossed arms or feet.

9. For a standing position

Do not remain immobile. Move naturally, move from time to time. You should never turn your back on the audience, even if you are writing to do it from the side.

10. Control the distance with the interlocutor

Come closer if you feel comfortable. If the other person backs up, don't step forward again.

11. Use the mirror technique

Subtly imitate others' body language (facial expressions, gestures, posture, tone of voice…).

How Non-Verbal Communication Can Go Wrong with Small Talk in an Office

Nonverbal communication has several layers and depending on the social environment in which you move. It is understood in one way or another. There is no dictionary with uniform translations of nonverbal messages.

The way you handle your body language may or may not affect your colleagues in an office. Why do I say it? The reason is simple. Certain raw emotions are not expressed with the same facial expression, gestures, etc. in everyone.

So, what should you do?

Stress management

Try to keep your stress level low. If you are under pressure, you will only have at your disposal a restricted range of mental resources. If you are stressed, it is very likely that you misinterpret non-verbal signals or even go unnoticed.

Development of emotional awareness

Only if you are aware of your feelings and if you know how

they affect you will you be able to interpret the body language of others correctly. Every so often, it would help if you took the time to investigate what affects your feelings, your posture, your facial expression, your gestures, and the modulation of your voice have.

The importance of context

Not only does cultural context matter, but situational and individual context also plays a vital role in evaluating non-verbal messages. For example, a hunched posture can indicate a lack of self-confidence, as long as it is not due to back problems. Crossed arms can indicate rejection, but some people cross their arms very often out of habit.

Tips for non-verbal communication at work

If you don't pay any attention to non-verbal messages in everyday communication at work, sooner or later, you will run into difficulties. And, to be successful at work, not only specialized practical knowledge matters. The so-called interpersonal skills, such as social skills, also matter. Above all, if you hold a position with people under your charge, it is essential that you know how to treat your employees. If you can read the non-verbal signals of your colleagues, partners, and clients, and if you consciously control your non-verbal communication, you have a good chance of being successful in your professional career.

As we have already discussed, it is tough to offer universal advice to interpret and use non-verbal messages. However, if we focus exclusively on the European and North American contexts, recommendations can be made on how non-verbal communication can give a more confident image or arouse sympathy.

Adapt to the non-verbal behavior of the interlocutor. It is only applicable if the interlocutor follows the basic rules of education. If your interlocutor starts screaming and fidgeting, you should not reflect that behavior. In everyday situations, you gain the other party's trust if you adapt slightly to your interlocutor in intonation, body language, and facial expression. This type of behavior is unconsciously valued as "something in common" and encourages the other party to be more open to your interventions.

The correct distance. Each person has a personal space in which only good friends and family can enter. You must not enter that area without permission. An average talking distance is between 60 and 150 cm. Depending on the confidence, you can vary the length.

Check your sitting posture. It does not matter if you are in a job interview or a work meeting: if you want to convey an image of security, use the entire surface of the seat, do not sit on the edge of the chair, because you will imply that you are about to leave or even that you want to run away. Maintain an upright but not stiff posture. Do not lean back in the chair and do not stick to the back. These positions can interpret as a lack of interest or arrogance. Lean forward a little from time to time to convey attention and, as far as possible, do not feel in an utterly frontal position concerning your interlocutor. This position generates a particular climate of confrontation. An angle between 30 and

60 degrees is considered ideal.

The importance of eye contact. Eye contact is one of the most important nonverbal cues. It helps you create a compelling, open, and trustworthy image. However, you should not look at your interlocutor in the eye for more than 3 seconds. If not, your gaze will appear stiff, and instead of confidence will cause discomfort.

Stable standing position. If you are standing, you will convey confidence as long as the posture is natural. The feet should be in line with the hips, and the arms should hang slightly to the sides. Contrary to what some experts claim, you don't need to distribute your body weight on both legs continually. It is not a negative thing if you always lean more on one leg than the other. On the contrary: a support leg change can increase your comfort level, giving you a more confident image.

Chapter 8. Non-Verbal Communication and the Social Code

In the previous chapter, we have seen that Many gestures used daily are common in most countries. However, others can mean different things, depending on where we are.

The verbal component is used to communicate information, and the non-verbal part to express emotional states and attitudes.

> these universal basics
> The basic gestures are usually the most universalized:
> move your head to affirm or deny something
> frown in anger
> a shrug of shoulders indicating that we do not understand or understand something

Other times, some gestures are inherited from the animal kingdom, such as showing teeth as a sign of anger (aggressiveness).

Who are the best non-verbal communicators?

Precisely for this reason, the best non-verbal communicators are aware of their body language, people who can monitor their behavior, and gauge its effect on others. Although they are usually observant people, there is no exact scientifically established profile, with a broad perspective, and open to new experiences and realities. Traits like emotional stability and empathy also help.

It may be easier to recognize them in the world of art and communication, but they occur in the same way in all professions. Some studies show that the most influential and persuasive people have a great awareness of their own and other people's body language, regardless of the professional field in which they have succeeded. It is a fundamental condition for success.

Therefore, becoming a good non-verbal communicator requires developing self-awareness of bodily behavior, in the same way, elite athletes improve proprioception to recognize the position and conditions of their musculature. The good news is that both skills can be developed with training. Also, we can do it on our own and at any time and circumstance.

It is a matter of concentration. And to focus attention on the main channels of body language, seeking their consistency and synchronization with the words.

Even if you know what a particular gesture can mean, do not make the mistake of interpreting it in isolation; it is easy for you to be wrong. Gestures can be faked, but not the whole-body acts in the same way. Eyebrows, laughter, the pupil of the eyes, and other small details surely give us away.

As a general rule, when we are lying or forcing a situation, the body gives us away. That is why personal cases are better-resolved face-to-face than by telephone and other means where the body can be hidden and lose an essential part of the message (the non-verbal part).

Although the topic is broad and could last for hundreds of pages, we have already put the main gestures and attitudes to help us in our daily lives and business. Most of the gestures and movements that we use regularly are conditioned by the environment in which we grew up.

It should be mentioned that cultural nuances are of great importance in body language. The family environment also has an evident influence on our behavior and our way of "speaking with the body." Therefore, you cannot miss the social code when talking about body language.

The meaning of the 'OK' gesture

The "OK" sign, OK (Wikipedia) with various theories about its origin, although the most accepted one of our kind visitors informed us is a deformation of the expression "all correct" in "all correct" that appeared in some newspapers Americans and Canadians during the 19th century.

Another theory is that it comes from the opposition to the meaning of "KO" (Knock Out). It means that everything is correct, although in certain countries, homosexuality is referred to by the similarity of the circle formed with the fingers, and in other countries, it is used to indicate something null, invalid, zero, or nothing at all.

Other authors affirm that the OK symbol comes from '0 kills', with no deaths in the front, used in the American Civil War.

The gesture of the 'V' of victory

The well-known sign of the "V", as a symbol of victory or triumph, popularized by Winston Churchill in World War II, does not mean the same thing. If it is done with the palm facing outwards, it means victory, that with the palm inwards, that means an obscene insult.

Interestingly, on the African continent, the "V" sign does not usually mean anything special in most of the countries of that continent. Making the "V" sign would only mean that we want to order two units of something.

In the UK, and generally in Anglo-Saxon culture, making the symbol of victory with the palm facing inward is an offensive gesture.

In other cultures, doing this with a gesture with the index and middle fingers can mean 'to put the horns.'

If you do the "V" with your fingers pointing to your eyes, it could mean I'm watching you; I'm watching you.

Obscene gestures are as common as positive gestures and are also part of non-verbal language.

When it comes to offending, sexual "cutting" and obscene gestures are the ones that irritate and annoy people the most.

Thumb down or thumb down: popularized globally by Facebook

Another well-known gesture is the thumb up or down, which

indicates agreement or disagreement. But in some countries, it is used to insult, as in Greece, and in others, it only means number one, as in many English-speaking countries (USA, New Zealand, Australia, etc.).

There are many variants of gestures with this finger, such as the hand's well-known form to "hitchhike," but we will not elaborate any further.

Personal space and social distance

We know how far to approach a person to chat, introduce them, etc. All people, according to recent studies and according to Allan Pease, have our territories very well defined:

- The intimate area, up to 50 centimeters away, where the closest people (family, close friends, etc.) approach.

- The personal zone up to 125 centimeters, approximately the distance used in meetings, work, and social environment.

- The social area, up to 2 or 3 meters, more or less, which is used with people outside our environment (the postman, an electrician, etc. and people on public roads).

Haptic

Haptics defines the touch and its influence on the way we relate. Touch gesture is essential when establishing intimacy, denotes commitment, and reveals highly sensitive information, such as dominance in the interaction. Touch has its power when it comes to influencing others' behavior, as occurs between doctors and patients. Physical contact has a marked cultural component: in Latin and Arab countries, it is much greater, for example, than in North America or Japan. A brief and light touch on "unencumbered" areas of the body (arms, shoulders, and upper back) can be the ultimate in establishing a good relationship.

Proxemic

It is the most direct channel of body language when it comes to showing ourselves close or distant. Proxemics has its origin in anthropology, and it informs us of the use of space in interaction. Some authors divide the distance between individuals into intimate (-45 cm), personal (between 45 cm and 120 cm), social (+120 cm), and public (+360 cm), depending on the type of relationship. The truth is that each person has their own space, and it can also vary according to their mood or environmental circumstances. The important thing is two things: 1º) The easiest way to show ourselves close is to approach our interlocutor physically, and 2nd) We must pay close attention to any sign of discomfort that our approach generates.

The issue of distances is of great importance when establishing contact or conversation with another person. Many people do not like that others "invade" their territory or personal zone. It has never happened to her that a person leans back to maintain a comfortable distance for her. These situations are highly variable depending on the environment (rural or urban) and depending on the situation. Those who have grown up in sparsely populated areas (rural centers) tend to have wider distances in their regions (both intimate, personal, and social) than those who were born in environments with a higher population density (generally urban centers).

The seven uses of body language

The influence of non-verbal behavior on human interaction is indisputable. Mastering body language is especially useful in some functions of socialization. These are just a few:

1. Communicate our identity.
2. To Inform others about our ability to relate.
3. Three, achieve precision and understanding.
4. Four Manage interaction.
5. Five Convey emotions and feelings.
6. Influence others and ourselves.
7. Produce deception.

The 7 main areas of application of body language

Mastering non-verbal behavior techniques are applicable in all areas of knowledge and any site of private and professional life. Hence the growing interest in the correct handling of body language. These are just some of the areas of application where it is particularly useful:

1. Communication and personal relationships
2. Teaching and training
3. Health and therapy
4. Security and forensic techniques
5. Negotiation and conflict resolution
6. Marketing and customer service
7. Human resources and personnel selection

We cannot know what a person thinks through their non-verbal behavior, but body language allows us to infer how they feel, what traits dominate their personality, or what their intentions are, information that is sometimes much more valuable than words. As with verbal communication, we must be very precise in expressing our body language and flexible in interpreting someone else's, always conditioned by various intrinsic and environmental factors that sometimes escape our ability to perceive.

The Factual Information Level

Everything you do or stop doing with your body is reflected in your voice. Starting with your posture: whether you are standing in front of the public or sitting in a chair in a radio studio if you remain upright and looking straight ahead, it will give you greater credibility, and whoever listens to you will perceive that you have mastered the subject.

The way you move also influences the way your message gets through. If you walk with a firm step on the stage, you will give energy and go to your words without moving excessively and supporting yourself with hand gestures.

That is, non-verbal communication can alter the message if it is not done correctly.

The Self-revealing or Self-disclosure Level

What are self-disclosures?

Self-disclosures are personal information that you offer to one or more people when you want to establish a powerful - emotional bond. In a way, it means expressing feelings, desires, likes, fantasies, long-term goals, procrastination, etc. Correctly and without excesses.

To carry out self-disclosures, there are many topics, such as family, city of origin, way of life and plans, points of view about marriage and children, reactions and discomfort, personal fears, thoughts about the old belief in God, life or death, drugs, triumphs and failures, old love affairs, moments of anguish, etc.

Suppose you want to communicate with someone, you must first consider not to rush when it comes to intimacies. People may feel uncomfortable if they are besieged in a short space of time with very intimate questions or self-disclosures. Wait for the right moment for it.

Common problems in self-disclosure

Project a false image

> You may find yourself rejected because the other person does not like this "perfect self" that you present.
> You may be drawn to a positive image, but you know yourself that this is not you.
> Sooner or later, the lie can be discovered.

They don't believe us

To increase the chances that they will judge us, we must:

> Be specific in describing the sensations
> Reveal some negative aspect of oneself
> Let yourself be convinced: instead of immediately stating an opinion, discuss with the interlocutor the pros and cons of the problem to finally draw a conclusion
> That there is no ambiguity when expressing your own opinion: Do not do it in the third person and with questions, but in the first person and with affirmative sentences
> Do not speak little for fear of boring the other person

Revealing private information about ourselves to another person is a very effective assertive technique in social conversation and when a conflict arises between ourselves and another person.

Voluntary self-disclosure should not be confused with the act of vomiting self-deprecating confessions of an involuntary, automatic, and quasi-conditioned type.

Chapter 9. Be a Good Storyteller

Being a good narrator telling the story is a fundamental factor when writing, whether it is a novel or a short story.

It is not about deciding whether the story will be told in the first or third person. You must also know what information you will have and what degree of involvement you will relate to the story. How to be a good storyteller? Let's see how below.

1. Use the protagonist's name sparingly

Example:

Ernst knew that he could not tell the truth to his wife. Ernst's wife was an old-fashioned person, and she was going to shout to heaven. Ernst had to do everything possible not to find out what had happened.

This example is a bit extreme, but it helps you to illustrate what you want to explain. If you're looking to improve your story, don't abuse your main character's name.

To improve a story, try not to let the main character's name slip through every step. It is enough that you mention it from time to time.

2. Reduce the feelings of the secondary characters

You must deal primarily with the protagonist. But many times, the storyteller ends up talking about the ideas, feelings, emotions, and thoughts of the secondary characters.

You will see it better with an example.

Gabby stopped at the entrance of the room. From there, she could make out Diane and Lucy, who were talking to each other. They were indeed commenting on every detail of the dresses of the women around them. Diane considered herself the ultimate connoisseur of fashion since she had returned from Italy. She was aware of all the trends and dressed like a costume. She thought that this way, she managed to attract the eyes of everyone around her because she loved being the center of attention. Gabby sighed and turned around. She did not want to talk to Diane and Lucy. She preferred to go out on the terrace to take the cool.

In this fragment, the narrator pauses for several sentences to talk about Diane. He leaves Gaby, his protagonist, at the door and stops talking about focusing on a secondary character.

The narrator tells us many things about Diane while omitting why Gabby does not want to talk to the women in the room, which prompts her to go out on the terrace.

The correct thing, on the contrary, would be to keep the focus on Gaby.

Gabby stopped at the entrance of the room. From there, she could make out Diane and Lucy, who were talking to each other. She did not talk to anyone. She preferred to go out on the terrace to take the fresh air.

An even more suitable option to improve the story would relate the information about Diane to Gaby herself. That would help the reader better understand, by contrast, the peculiarities of the character of the protagonist.

Gaby stopped at the entrance of the room. From there, she could make out Diane and Lucy, who were talking to each other. They were indeed commenting on every detail of the dresses of the women around them. She could not bear that Diane considered herself the ultimate connoisseur of fashion. She was always aware of all the trends and dressed like a costume. She was frivolous. She thought that this way, she managed to attract the eyes of everyone around her because she loved being the center of attention. Gabby sighed and turned around. She didn't want to talk to Diane and Lucy. Stealthily, she went out onto the terrace to get some fresh air.

This version better explains why Gabby does not want to talk to the salon women, and it is understood that she chooses to go out for a cold drink. The frivolous character of Diane is also opposed to that of Gaby, which allows the reader to know more about the protagonist. Diane is frivolous, while Gabby is not. Diane enjoys attracting attention. Gabby prefers to sneak in so she won't be seen.

3. Find the voice of your narrator

When writing, you must take care to give each character their voice. A doctor will not speak the same as a teenager. So, you have to take care that each character has its register distinguished from the rest.

Well, the same happens when you narrate. The voice is vital because it acts as a filter of the story for the reader. It is their words that present and unfold the story, so you need to carefully choose how you will express yourself and the way you will tell what happens.

Several aspects condition that voice:

> Who are you?

It happens as with the characters: if you are an educated person, you will not express yourself the same as a person without studies. If you are a child, you cannot express yourself as an adult.

> Whether or not you intervene in the development of the story

If your character is also one of the characters in the story, you should speak when narrating as she does when intervening in a dialogue. You cannot change the record based on acting as a narrator or as a character.

If the story affects you closely, your way of narrating and expressing yourself will be different (closer, more vivid) than an objective third-person narrator, whose tone will be more impersonal.

> What perspective do you give to the story?

The narrator can tell a story from a humorous, dramatic,

mysterious perspective ... Depending on it, his voice will vary.

How much do you know?

Not just how much you know about the story you tell, but in general.

For example, if you are a child, there will be many things that you cannot explain well, simply because you do not know them.

If you put these three simple tips into practice, you will see you improve your story significantly.

Holding interest

Interest is the most precious asset in these times in which, between the internet and social networks. The temptations to kidnap it have multiplied. So, you must know how to show interest and hold others' attention before and while you tell the story. There are several ways to do it. But one of the most real is by using the name. Everyone's favorite word is their name. We can hear it even at a Rock concert with the speaker close by. So, you can use this when you see that you have lost the attention of the interlocutor. It's that simple. You just have to say their name.

Building connections

The story must be relevant to the audience, but how do you get an exciting connection? The connections must generate a question in the receiver. Healthy and meaningful questions for your audience lead to a more excellent bond. And a question or connection week for them will make them disconnect.

Summarize

US President Woodrow Wilson once said:

"If I have to prepare a 10-minute speech, I need a week of preparation. On the other hand, if the speech is to last 1 hour, it did not need any preparation."

The more we have to summarize our ideas, the more difficult it becomes. However, it is a great exercise to fine-tune the message of your story. Suppose that it takes you 15 minutes to tell your story and propose to shorten the message to convey your ideas in just 5 minutes.

You never know how much attention time they will grant you. So, start with the most important. Try to make each part of your story arouse curiosity in the other person so that they keep the interest to continue listening to you.

A Satisfying Conclusion

A satisfying conclusion corresponds to the final stage of your story. That is the most relevant information or proposed as 'new' in the story.

Therefore, the conclusion is directly related to something previously admitted, proposed, or evidenced in the introduction and development of your story.

Chapter 10. Making Genuine Connections with People

The human connection does not require magic or tricks. It requires honesty and the ability to give yourself to the other from simplicity, emotional balance, and that humble empathy that looks at the other with interest in reading needs and virtues.

We have all wanted to decipher that mystery that builds human relationships, that enigma that configures the psychology of connection, and that fascinates us so much.

Now, you may wonder what 'connecting' really means? It means; "putting two things (devices, systems) in contact so that a reaction is generated between them or some kind of communication." It is clear without a doubt that people are not machines but curiously, our brain does present an electrical activity.

The human being connects through emotion. Each of us reacts and transform when we connect with certain people who are stimulating to us. Therefore, our relationships result from a fascinating mechanism of chemical and electrical reactions that help us create bonds.

The human being needs these connections not only to share

spaces, interests, or objectives. There is an inherent need to socialize and find reference figures who bring us friendship, affection, and unconditional support.

So, ask yourself those following questions.

> What do I need to connect with people better?
> What must I do to create impact, excite, and leave that indelible mark with which to build lasting relationships?

Here are four ways to practice them:

1. Take the time

Rule to break: Move very quickly from person to person at networking events.

The best members of the family sit, listen, and repeat what you say, showing empathy and understanding. To strengthen professional bonds, you must take the time to understand others' experiences and challenges, using active listening skills.

Action: Check your clock on the door and look for quality conversations, not quantity.

2. Let conversations flow naturally

Rule to break: Get your list of questions ready.

At family gatherings, we generally go to those members who provide light and easy-going conversation, avoiding those members who ask question after question.

Our networking uses this fact and encourages you to start a fluent conversation and not like an interview with a list of questions. Therefore, conversations grow naturally, and the relationship is strengthened based on trust and mutual respect.

Action: Let the conversation flow. Be gentle and not intense.

3. Help others first

Rule to break: Give and receive

Sometimes to promote a family, we must help others before ourselves. Put merely, reciprocity doesn't happen immediately. The coaches and recruiters we work with often put others before themselves. Ultimately, they get advice, support, and more opportunities than they ever had before. This long-term benefit is based on trust and a desire to support those people in your network, helping others first.

Action: Be altruistic. Expect not to receive an immediate benefit.

4.Connect with non-influential people

Rule to break: Make connections with speakers and recognized people.

At conferences and events, speakers, event coordinators, and influencers are busy. Many people try to connect with these industry celebrities, making each connection attempt less memorable for them. Instead, our networking builds solid relationships with people before becoming celebrities or influential people in the interest sector. It's like building a relationship as a child with a cousin growing up to become the CEO of a Fortune 500 company. Instead of looking for the industry celebrity, look for people who are not influential and have strong leadership potential. As they rise throughout your career, they will take you with them.

Action: Seek potential, not fame or fortune.

There is power in a real and authentic relationship. Restoring warmth and familiar social skills in networking can help you grow personally and professionally in the long run. At your next conference or event, build relationships like a family member, and create lasting relationships that will support you throughout your career.

Signs You Are Connecting with Someone

The people with whom you maintain an emotional connection make you feel calm, comfortable in the interaction. That connection makes you learn about the life, recharge your energy, and be happier.

1. Understanding

Two people with this connection have the possibility of reaching very high levels of understanding. An understanding that is based on empathy facilitates, for example, help, listening, or comfort.

2. The instant connection

Building and maintaining an emotional connection doesn't always need to build that relationship first. Sometimes it requires the match of personalities from the start. The link is thus instantaneous and can intensify further over time.

Even if you do not feel an emotional connection when meeting someone for the first time, that means that it can never arise between those two people. "Instantaneity" is a characteristic feature of emotional connection, but it does not determine, in any way, its development.

3. Personal growth

People who share an emotional connection grow personally and spiritually faster together. Thanks to that connection, these two people know perfectly what the other's concerns are and, generally, they share them. It fosters a positive environment that encourages both of you to grow in experiences.

It has a lot to do with communication. Dialogues between people with an emotional connection are often stimulating. They never stop learning from each other, whatever the topic of conversation.

4. Peace of mind

People with an emotional connection often feel at peace in this company. From that absence of stress, it is straightforward to distance yourself from problems and see them in perspective. That tranquility gives way to positive emotions, if not to a new view, allowing solving a particular issue.

5. The company

The connection is an excellent antidote to loneliness. The emotional connection covers us with a sense of company, regardless of the distance that separates us. Related to this with tranquility, we feel that we are present in the other's thoughts, that we exist beyond our physical limits.

In times of crisis, immensely, this feeling helps to find solutions. Without needing to ask for help, that person will do everything possible to be with you, listen to you, and support you when you need it most.

6. The fascination

We are fascinated by the people with whom we have such a special connection. We always find them interesting, and we are their biggest fans. Any triumph of people with an emotional connection is shared by the other sincerely, without envy, without judgment.

It does not mean that people with this connection are incapable of seeing the other's flaws. They are the ones who see them the most since they consider each other to be transparent. However, unlike other people, it is straightforward to talk about the other's defects and grow as a person, as we have already seen.

7. Empathy

The last important trait of emotional connection is empathy. As we have already seen, people who share this bond do not always need to verbalize their concerns: they can extract others' personal needs through conversation. The ease of putting yourself in the place of the other makes the relationship stronger.

Other tips on emotional connection

When the relationship with another person already exists, you can also nurture the connection. It is accomplished through the conscious practice of the hallmarks of emotional connection.

So, it could be easier for the other person to feel that our concern is real, which we express to help more and better. In many cases, only with this gesture will we get the other to lower their anxiety one degree and improve communication.

Finally, highlight the importance of emotionally engaging responses: if someone transmits an experience to us, we will do well to worry about what happened in that event, but we will do it even better if we also pay attention or can read how it felt the person at that time.

Chapter 11. Ending Small Talks Gracefully

Be in a hurry and meet that friend or relative that you haven't seen in a long time and want to give you an update on their life ... Or just have nothing more to say: How to end a conversation without cutting someone off or making them feel uncomfortable?

It has happened to you that you meet someone and don't know how to cut the talk. Below, what to say and how to say it in these situations.

You must always keep in mind cordiality and assertiveness, taking into account the context and the person you are with to know how it is appropriate to act.

The main thing for the other person to believe you and allow you to end the conversation is saying why and always being kind, making the other person feel that you have spent a good time talking with him and that the reason is not a lack of interest for which you are going.

How to end a small talk?

Tip #1: The positive comment

It's almost a direct denial that the other person is dull or making you desperate. Include the person's name to make the farewell more personal.

• Mary: "I was delighted to talk to you, and I appreciate all the ideas you gave me."

Tip #2: The Summary/Plan

Going over the key points of the conversation will make the other person feel heard, and he/she will know that you paid attention to him/her; and if you mix it with a plan of action, it will signal that the conversation is closed.

• Ethan: "Thank you very much for clarifying all the points, I will review the contract again, and I will tell you what my decision was."

Tip # 3: The credible excuse

Always take care, to be honest. The idea is that you indicate that for urgent reasons. There are duties or people you have to attend to, and you should leave but not because that person is boring you or is not essential. Offer an apology, easing the situation by feeling sorry for having to leave.

Julie: "I am very sorry to have to go because I was pleased to have seen you, but…"

Tip # 4: invite a second conversation

Johnson: "I was very pleased to see you. I hope we can talk again soon. I will leave you my information or pass me yours so that we do not leave this issue unfinished."

Tip # 5: use body language

> See the watch or phone
> Stand up
> Look at the door
> Put your things away

You have to take care

> That your non-verbal language does not reflect impatience or despair (unless you want to communicate that), always give away!
> Don't be too blunt by cutting off the conversation suddenly.
> If you say things like "I don't want to hold you any longer," "I see you are busy, but it was good to see you," you can get caught up in the conversation again…

Often, the meetings, conversations, or impromptu talks at a networking event take longer than stipulated, and sometimes, the way you end can seem rude. So, I will give you some phrases that you can use for some widespread occasions.

On the phone

> I have another call in a couple of minutes; Thank you very much for contacting me. We talk later
> My battery doesn't have much of a charge, so I'll have to hang up. Have a great day
> I think we talked about all the issues we had pending, so I will let it go. Thanks for the productive conversation
> I can't believe it's so late already. I'm sure you are busy, so I'll let you go. If you need help, just let me know

At a networking event

> Excuse me. I have to go to the dresser. It was a delight to meet you
>
> It was a pleasure chatting with you. I will connect on LinkedIn to find out about your news
>
> Excuse me. I have to go. It was a pleasure, and I hope we can meet again very soon. Do you have a business card?
>
> I will share with other guests, but first of all, allow me to introduce you to a person

In the office

> I have to go back to my job to finish a project. Let's catch up on a happy hour
>
> I know you have a crazy schedule, so I'll let you come back
>
> I would love to know more about her work, so we will catch up when we have more.
>
> I have a piece of mail to send before lunch, so they will have to excuse me

In a meeting

> I think we have caught up with the entire schedule. If no one else has anything to say, see you next week
>
> There's another meeting in this conference room, so we should clean up and let the other guys in.
>
> Good to have finished 15 minutes early. I'm going to end sending some emails
>
> Are you going to your office? I will walk with you
>
> Thank you all for the very productive meeting we had. I'll

> send you some notes that I took later

In a video conference

> I appreciate the time you had to talk to me. Have a nice day
> Your ideas look very promising. I can't wait for them to materialize
> I will have the answers to your questions as soon as possible so that I will leave. Greetings
> I can't believe the time has passed so fast. Do you mind if I keep finishing my to-do list?

Simple steps to complete a conversation

> Interrupt the interlocutor: "Wait," "Great!" "Sorry, but...".
> Say what you should be doing instead of talking: "I don't want to interrupt you, but I'm late for work," "If you don't mind, I'll go get something at the bar."
> End the conversation with pleasant and sincere words: "It was a pleasure to see you!" "Thank you, it was interesting to chat" "I hope you have a good time here."

Don't make excuses. Speak calmly, confidently, and with a smile. 99% of people will understand and won't insist on continuing the conversation. If someone gets angry or offended, well, you did everything you could. You were courteous, honest, and tried to say something nice. You should not strive to please everyone without exception.

Making an Excellent Last Impression

It is possible to stop a conversation without spoiling a relationship delicately. But giving another person the last impression is something that you owe a lot to consider. In this section, I will tell you how to do so.

1. Stop your interlocutor with a gesture

First, open your mouth slightly, leaning towards the person, as if you were about to say something ("fish" gesture). If this doesn't make your interlocutor stop, at least he/she will finish his/her sentence faster. In case that doesn't help, reach out your hand towards this person, stopping him/her ("separating" gesture). Finally, touch his/her hand. Usually, a touch silences even the most talkative for a moment. Taking advantage of the pause, you can change the conversation topic and then end it without problems.

2. Admit your "incompetence."

If you are not interested in a conversation, calmly admit that you do not know about it. You can say, "Unfortunately, I can't keep talking, I'm not up to date on political developments," "Admit it, I'm terrible at talking about floriculture," or "Excuse me, I'm not keeping up with the latest fashion trends."

3. Mention your principles

If people ask uncomfortable questions, rush to share new gossip, or raise an unpleasant topic, you have the right to clearly state your position: "I have a rule, I don't talk about my personal life (parenting, religious affiliation)." Usually, the mention of personal principles causes respect, and the interlocutor changes the subject.

4. Say a compliment

A long monologue from a colleague or relative can be stopped by saying something nice or "remembering" exciting news: "I understand you; this is a challenging situation ... Oh, I just noticed something ... did you start putting on makeup in such a way? Different? Do you have a new dress/bag/earring? By the way, did you hear that ...?

5. Interrupt not the interlocutor, but yourself

If someone tells you many stories about his/her own life, "join" your interlocutor with a phrase such as "Yes, I also had a similar situation," or "Don't tell me, the same thing happened to me," and start to tell something over you. In between, remember that you lost track of time: "Oh, I talk so much! I'm not going to distract you anymore, I apologize!". When you interrupt yourself, and not the interlocutor, he/she does not experience psychological discomfort when ending a conversation.

6. Ask what you can do to help

If a person complains about their life non-stop, ask him/her if and how you can help. It will show your interest and, at the same time, interrupt the flow of complaints. As a general rule, disgruntled ones simply seek out sensitive ears, so he/she will reply that nothing can help his/her situation. Now you can close the topic by saying: "Let me know if you need anything."

7. Leave with a pretext

In a neutral setting (at a conference, party), you can always escape a cheeky interlocutor by asking where the bathroom is or offering to get a drink. If a coworker comes to your office, talks, or feels like leaving, walk them out yourself: while you continue the conversation, leave the table (for example, with a cup to serve tea) and make some Steps. The person will be forced to follow you, you will take her to her place of work, and then you will calmly return to yours.

8. Use the "fake call" application

If the other person is impenetrable and is eager to show you the 500 selfies, he/she took on vacation, use the "Fake Call" app. Pretend someone is calling you, allowing you to escape without saying anything.

Chapter 12. Developing Your Conversations Skills

Talk, chat, debate, discuss, and dialogue. If we stop to analyze each of these words' meanings, we will realize that all in one way or another designate speaking that two or more people carry out and usually have the objective of exchanging ideas, thoughts, and knowledge on specific topics.

The act of starting a conversation can be done in several ways. The most traditional is in which a face-to-face dialogue is established through oral or sign language. Technology is often the mediator of conversion in these times. Through it, conversations can be made in writing, such as correspondence, email, instant messaging, or video calls.

Differentiating ourselves from the rest of the animals by establishing the verbal language makes it the way to communicate par excellence, but talking demands from us a responsibility with the other. It is vital to have the power and knowledge to determine when a conversation is not working and what actions we should take to improve it. In this writing, we aim to provide some elements that should not be said when we start a conversation.

There are a group of critical elements that make up what a healthy conversation could say:

Content: what we say. Although this represents only about 7% of what we pay attention to, still it matters

Process: how we say it. It is estimated that 55% of the process is carried out through non-verbal communication, with 38% being only the vocal tone

Timing: when we say it. It greatly influences how we process information

By far, the essential thing is permission: Are we talking to each other or each other?

Here are ten things not to say in conversation:

- Take it easy
- just relax
- Do not Cry
- You are very sensitive
- You're overreacting
- Everything happens for a reason
- When I was your age
- Good luck with that
- Other people's lives are worse than yours
- Don't take it so seriously

Dealing with Awkward Silences

It doesn't matter if you're shy or not. We always come across conversations that get awkward because we don't know how to follow the line of it. We've all had that experience. And we don't always know what to do or how to react to an uncertain situation. Fortunately, there are simple tricks to solve it and become the most talkative being in the world:

Give short and straightforward answers

Every day you have conversations with so many different people about so many other things that we often do not even remember what we say or talk to us. It does not mean that many of the conversations have to be meaningful; That is why it is okay for you not to know what to say because, most likely, no matter what you say or if you do not say anything at all, it will probably all be forgotten.

So why is there so much talk if our conversations are not meaningful? We like to feel connected to each other, and chatting with people helps us understand each other. The purpose of having a conversation is, pure and simple, to keep the conversation going.

You do not need to prepare attractive or intelligent answers

For example, if the person you are chatting with talks to you about unfamiliar topics, you don't need to be an expert to express an opinion. Just say what you think, and now, no one should criticize or judge your knowledge, and you could even take the conversation from another perspective and be happy that you are talking with someone regardless of the content.

Listen to what the other is saying, and try to relate it to something else

Another trick is to associate the conversation. In other words, every discussion generates inspiration and allows you to know exciting things that you may not even know. You wander and move on with what you have to say.

Ask questions and let the other person talk more

If you don't feel super comfortable with the conversation, let your curiosity come out and not be afraid to ask. Let the other person speak and share his/her excitement or enthusiasm with you. It shows that you respect the other person and that you are enjoying the conversation. People will generally be happy that you hear them and will want to share more with you.

Share your little stories with others

If you still feel an uncomfortable silence, do not worry: you can always share a little about yourself, it is the best topic you handle, and this way, you will make others interested in you, generating trust.

Starting One-on-One Conversations

Start easy

Some formulas are like Coca-Cola; they work for sure. Questions like "What's up?" "How is your day?" or "Hi, how are you?" they assure an answer type: "good, and you?". That is the answer you are looking for. This study showed that by answering "okay," that person will be more willing to engage in conversation and engage in social behavior.

If someone answers you: "the truth is that I'm pretty bad," run foolishly.

You don't need exciting conversation starters; they will give them to you

One of the most frequent questions when starting a conversation is: "What am I talking about? I don't know any interesting or funny topics! "

It's a wrong question.

What you should ask yourself is: "How can I get them to talk about themselves?"

How do we get it?

My favorite phrase is: "Oh yeah?" Using this question after a statement from your interlocutor ensures that they keep talking to add more details.

You can also use others such as: "tell me more" or use classic questions such as: where, when, with whom you did that.

You don't want to look impressive. It does not work

One technique that is often used to appear attractive is to associate with well-known characters. Do not do it. Using the classic "I know Smith Angel" will not help you make friends, quite the opposite.

The paradox is that you tend to seem more impressive when you care about others.

Arouse that genuine interest you have inside to know more about them. Ask questions fearlessly but carefully.

Look for and point out the similarities

The similarity is compelling. We like more names that resemble ours, people who support our team, or those who live in the same city.

The similarity is so powerful that it is one of the foundations of persuasion.

When you find a source of similarity, delve into it—linking it with the example from before.

- What problem have your children given you this week?
- Well, look, the little one has taken to painting and has scribbled all over the living room wall with the pen.
- He, he, it happened to me too. I still remember how angry I got. Hey, what have you done?
- Well, look…

One way to generate similarity is by making your interlocutor feel that you are part of the same group. Maybe you were both born in the same city, you went to the same school, or you both follow the same person on Instagram. If you discover it, you will soon generate sympathy, which will help to maintain a pleasant conversation.

Having Deeper Conversations

People need to have deep conversations regularly to feel good. Having someone with whom to engage in that peaceful dialogue that helps us reach the basement of our emotions not only pleases and relaxes but is also a gift for our brain. It is how stress is reduced and how the most enriching human connection is built.

Henry James used to say that there are two kinds of people in life, those we trust and those we don't. In reality, we could also point out that we have two types of people in our day to day, those with whom it is possible to have an intimate and empathetic conversation and those with whom we simply limit ourselves to talking about superficial and anodyne things.

How to have deep conversations and make unforgettable encounters

Finding a topic of conversation: talking about something that just happened

Every time you start a conversation with a stranger or someone you don't know very well, one technique is to talk about something that just happened to you on the same day.

It allows you not to ask a direct question and gives them the possibility of returning an interrogation to answer or add what they know about the subject.

Don't underestimate the number of good conversations you can have by saying, "I just had the most incredible pasta dish I've ever eaten during my time in Italy!"

So don't forget to use narrative elements to involve your auditor:

describe the context, the people involved, what they look like, what happened, and what was the difficulty.

Approach the conversation openly

This point has to do with conversations where you don't necessarily have the same perspective. My advice is not to avoid different topics or opinions because it makes discussions more prosperous and enjoyable.

If you don't agree with something, listen to the other person and consider their perspective, instead of pretending to win the conversation or be right, set your goal to understand another person better and understand a different perspective.

For example, if you are used to arguing with your best friend in politics, try to deepen the conversation by listening to each other carefully and being willing to take their point of view into account.

Raises personal issues

It may seem obvious to create a strong bond with someone, but it is not apparent when putting it into practice.

Indeed, asking personal questions works best in a relaxed context with a friend, we already know more or less.

It is the best way to get to know someone better in a more profound way. Personal questions also show that you are interested and want to hear what the other has to say.

I will return to this topic later in my guide but never be afraid to ask questions too soon, as long as you feel that you are not bothering the other person (they do not need to be too intrusive either. It is up to you to "feel" to your neighbor).

Breaking the ice: avoid overly banal greetings

From the beginning of the conversation, you can avoid the first "small talks" and demarcate yourself from the greeting's usual formulas. For example, asking: "what do you do?" You put your interlocutor in a 'dead-end' where she can only tell you about her work.

One way around this question would be, for example:

˜   What is it that makes you someone different?

˜   What is it that characterizes you?

It is sure to provoke a smile and surprise your interlocutor.

But these formulas are powerful. They touch directly on their fiber, what constitutes us, what makes us unique and different from others. You may even discover something a little crazy that others are unaware of: who knows. Maybe it's a doctor by day and a rock star by night?

If you already know the person, you can try breaking the ice with a trivial question like, "How did you spend the weekend? Or What's new?"

But generally, the answers are vague and in little detail.

That is why I recommend you better ask: What has been the best of your weekend? o Are you hoping to do something special this week?

In this way, your partner can tell you a story that will allow you to know more about him and motivate him.

These tips can also be applied when you ask what you do (among other things): do not just say that you are a student or Erasmus. You can liven up the conversation by adding details about something you have done related to your activity or stay.

In the same way, if you are asked what you do for fun or relaxation, tell about a recent experience that you have had enjoying your hobbies, whether it is having done a piano concert or 'jogging' in the park.

Ask questions about your life and experiences

Another effective way to address personal issues, without being too intrusive, is to ask the other about their experiences. It is better to approach positive experiences because, according to psychology, the other will associate this positive experience with you, leaving you in a perfect place.

To make this more concrete, here are some examples:

- How do you feel about having grown up in another country and having moved here?

- How was your trip to East Asia as a volunteer?

- How did you know that you wanted to become an English teacher in Japan?

- What is the most challenging obstacle you have had to overcome?

Try to establish a real relationship

You never need to force the conversation. Try to talk about something that the other person is passionate about, which interests you. This way, the relationship is real, and your partner will be more willing to talk in-depth about it.

Another psychological element to consider is not to assume the other is bored or not interested in the conversation. Because, well, this is going to affect the discussion and ruin it unconsciously.

And on the other hand, imagine that the other person is also interested in having deep conversations and having many things to teach you.

Discover your goals and your dreams

Asking someone about their goals is one way to learn how they want to progress. Knowing a person's goals and dreams can encourage them to open up to you and talk about things that touch their heart, ensuring a lively and exciting discussion.

They can be targets of different domains (concern for career, fitness, lifestyle, hobbies...)

Here are some concrete examples:

- What would you like to be in life?
- What goals would you like to achieve during the next 5 years?

Take an interest in their family

Family shapes people in significant ways and influences them throughout their lives. Learning to know someone's family can contribute a lot. You can start with basic questions to continue with more significant aspects.

For example, ask:

- How many brothers and sisters do you have?
- Do you get along with your family?
- What kind of relationship do you have?

But you must consider that not everyone likes to talk about their family. If the person seems unhappy or changes the subject, be respectful.

Ask questions about his/her career rather than about his/her job

Asking questions about someone's career is preferable from a professional perspective and can be an excellent way to approach someone. For someone who feels trapped in their work, talking about their studies and their expectations can be a step forward in encouraging them to realize that they have other options.

For example, if you want to have a conversation with a colleague, ask him/her what brought him/her here or what he/she likes the most. You can also ask him/her where he/she would like to go or what her career goal is.

On the contrary, if your interlocutor does not like his/her work too much, avoid this topic. You can try asking him/her questions about his/her hobbies. You can often learn more about a person by asking about their hobbies than their job.

Therefore, even if you work on the same thing, try to take your partner to a more personal level, moving away from professional topics.

Remember your previous conversations

One way to show respect for the person is to remind yourself of previous conversations and the important things.

For example, if you know that he/she has just returned from his/her Erasmus trip, ask her about that. It shows that you are listening to them and that you care about their life.

It can also help you understand her better and open the door to more conversations.

Here is a concrete example:

- How did the exam go? I know you have worked a lot.

Another advantage of recovering old songs is to start a feeling of nostalgia.

Recognizing old events remembering them is a sure way to inspire feelings of appreciation. According to a 'Clay Routledge' psychology study, it was revealed that commenting on shared moments between two people increases the sense of social connection and makes you more respectful of each other.

To delve into nostalgia, I recommend talking about your experiences growing up, childhood, and adolescence. It allows you to create an intimate bond with the other person. By expressing everything that you have felt during your youth or what has done you wrong as a child, you give the other a real idea of what has shaped you as an adult.

Ask open questions

A conversation is not about talking to someone: it is the conversation itself that must affect the person. You will learn more about each other's points of view and experiences by asking open and interesting questions. If the person is telling you something, chain them with an interrogation that encourages them to continue speaking.

The idea is to keep the questions open so that the other can continue as they wish. An in-depth conversation is difficult to develop from interrogations whose answer is only "yes" or "no" because we enter a deadlock.

It also allows for more information, allowing the other to explore and share their thoughts and opinions.

For example, instead of asking another Erasmus student: Do you like living in Italy? You can ask: How do you feel in your new city?

Or even questions like this:

- What did you think of this?
- What would you like to do?
- What are you thinking?

Follow up with more in-depth questions

Rather than scratch the surface of several different issues, feel free to ask for more information on the preceding answer and help the other to open up.

Simply put, if you ask a general question, follow it up with more specific questions. Your questions should engage the person and help create depth in the conversation.

For example, if someone talks about a travel memory, you can immediately ask them: How has this trip changed your life? o What have you gained from this experience?

Be careful, however, not to overlap question after question. It is not that the discussion turns into an interrogation or gives the impression of a police interrogation!

Ask the right questions that show that you are committed

One of the best ways to show your commitment is to establish a natural curiosity about what the other person says to you.

Be sure to ask at least one question before moving on to the next topic. Collecting details increases the chances that you can connect with the other. This phase also makes it possible to find a way to lend a hand, to help others (but I will talk about this again later).

In the same way, moderate the time you spend talking about yourself.

People spend about 60% of their time in conversation, talking about themselves, which causes the brain to release dopamine, and we feel good. But a deep conversation needs back and forth, balanced exchanges between two people. Therefore, take into account the exchange time and balance.

Find common interests and experiences

A simple and easy way to communicate with someone is to find common interests, hobbies, and experiences with the person you are talking to. Maybe you have grown up close to each other, attended the same university, or watched the same television broadcasts. Ask him what his route is and, if yours is similar, compare it!

Because it's no accident that dating sites bring people together based on what they have in common: Several studies say that common interests keep relationships healthy.

When two people have common interests, this creates less division and fewer differences between them.

For example, if your friend is sad because his Erasmus experience ends and you have had a similar experience, both of you can realize how difficult it is to get back into your routine and return to your country. Telling complicated relationships often brings meaning and comfort.

Even if you haven't had similar experiences, you can show that you understand and listen.

For example, you can try saying something like: I do not understand Chinese at all, but I am fascinated by people who understand it. It must have demanded much work!

When looking for common ground, don't expect deep themes to come to mind immediately. If you are not inspired, a trick is to talk about psychology or any other topic that concerns our behaviors, our ways of acting. Because in this domain, we are all together: we interact with other human beings, alongside other actions.

Give and ask for advice

This technique may demand a good deal of courage for some, but it is beneficial.

Asking for advice can also help you appear more competent and get the other person to become your ally.

Indeed, giving advice becomes one of the most potent forms of compromise between two people. From the moment you counsel a loved one about a challenge they are in, this means that you are prepared to be honest with them and that you care about them.

These two signals combined communicate a too high level of trust, creating a deeper level of proximity. Because trust between two people ultimately has results.

On the other hand, asking for advice takes you back to the previous point: it helps you express your vulnerability and favors intimacy.

But be careful not to abuse by giving unsolicited advice! It is necessary to have the person in front of you and check how they react.

Giving advice that the other person has not asked for can unleash a defensive attitude (based on the human need to maximize our freedom and our decision making).

If you have doubts about how the other will react to your advice, it is best to ask questions in advance and express empathy for their situation, for example: "It seems a difficult situation, have you thought about what you are going to do?

Show that you care about the other

An in-depth conversation does not necessarily have to be a long or lengthy conversation in detail. Show that you care about the other, support, and be willing to help.

Small gestures can mean a lot, so celebrate the person's successes and show them that you are here for them, especially when they are going through a difficult time.

For example, share your enthusiasm when you find out that he/she has obtained a scholarship. Or when he/she has passed his/her exams. Or when he/she has been accepted on an Erasmus trip. Offer him/her your support. Help in a meaningful way, either through a text message, email, or conversation in person.

Consider how you can add value to the discussion

It is essential to ask yourself how you can add value to someone through discussion. It can consist of information, reflections, advice … In short, useful things that the person does not know but that will be useful. You will be amazed at the number of occasions to connect with someone when you know their priorities.

On the other hand, a study has shown that happier people avoid small superficial conversations and have twice as many in-depth short talks as less happy people.

You have to remember to value others' time, using it wisely: to appreciate the time spent talking, ignoring the small conversations to go to the discovery of how you and your partner can help each other.

Do what can help you

Simply put, lending a hand will set you apart from the crowd in the other person's eyes. It doesn't matter what a conversation you have, whether you can help someone else, and most people don't keep their promises.

People will appreciate your relationship more if you stick with what you've suggested: a contact, something useful, specific information, or a fact.

Dopamine is released when we talk about ourselves and our experiences. Well, when something is shared with others (be it a profound secret, a dream, or an aspiration), our pleasure centers also light up, and another hormone called oxytocin is released. Another name for oxytocin? The love hormone because it plays a vital role in creating bonds between two people.

Making Conversation in Particular Situations

Friendly conversation

A friendly conversation is that a conversation, which generally has friendly and informal overtones, maintains with another individual or with several, who act as interlocutors, with the mission of commenting on a topic, putting it, or becoming aware of something between another question.

How to make a friendly conversation

~   Learn to put fear or shyness aside

Before starting a conversation, it is best to relax and take it easy. Ensure that everything goes very natural and keep in mind that it is normal for you to have doubts and fear rejection, especially if you do not know the other person. Be calm, courteous, and as secure in yourself as possible

~   If you don't see the person, it is best to introduce yourself

For that moment when you are going to start a conversation with a person you do not know, it is best to introduce yourself. It's a great way to break the ice and also shows you are outgoing and friendly. You can shake hands and smile at him. If that person is encouraged to give you a kiss or two, be receptive or receptive.

Ensure that during the first moments, the conversation is active, and there are no silences. They can be annoying. The usual thing is to talk about unimportant things. The rest will flow little by little. The important thing is to get to know the person without haste and to know if they have the same tastes and hobbies as you since this will make it easier to look for topics to talk about.

Avoid complicated topics and use cliches

In this case, it is essential not to go into topics such as politics or religion; it may be uncomfortable for the other person. Nor should we talk about clichés such as time, it is something too used, and it can be noticed that the conversation is being forced, and it shows that you are not too original.

You can have one or more topics of conversation prepared for these occasions. Look for something that you have much knowledge about that may be interesting. You can also talk about a movie you have seen an event you would like to go to.

Example;

- Albert: Hi Mary, how have you been?

- Mary: Very good! How are you?

- Albert: All good. I hadn't seen you for a long time.

- Mary: I was indeed traveling. I got to know several countries in Asia this last year.

- Albert: That sounds very interesting! Did you bring back memories?

- Mary: Yes, I brought a key ring from each country I visited.

Semi-formal conversation

An informal conversation is given when the people who participate in it carry out an exchange of information in a freeway, without taking care of forms or protocols. The people who participate in this type of conversation are few, and all are in the same circumstances. That is, there is no type of role or formal leadership in any of them. They all have the same right to speak and the same obligation to respect others. It is a free format and has no purpose.

This type of conversation is the one you have with friends, with people who have just met, or with a co-worker. The topics are diverse, and individual education rules only regulate it; the only law in an informal conversation is that speaking should be alternated between all participants.

Example;

- Hi Jean, how have you been?

- Well, Laurie, look, I introduce you to Carl, he's the classmate I told you about.

- Hi Carl.

- Hi Laurie, it's a pleasure to meet you.

- We sit down, says Jean.

- Yes, of course, - Carl and Laurie say almost in unison.

- Well, Jean, what can you tell me, how did your team do this weekend?

- Laurie, you couldn't let that go. Look, Carl, Laurie is a great soccer fan with the only fault of going to the wrong team. So, since my team lost this weekend, she'll be teasing all afternoon. By the way, she lost against Laura's favorite team.

- Well, here is something that you are not going to like Laurie, - said Carl - I also go to Jean's team.

- I already said that you couldn't be so perfect. You would have to have some defect - Laurie said in a mocking tone, and the three of them laughed at this comment.

Becoming Aware of Empathy

When you want to start a conversation, a simple "hello" is the easiest way to get in touch with someone. This strategy's danger is that it is straightforward to run out of topic to talk about since the greeting is empty of content. If you want to continue the conversation after the greeting, we will have to look more specifically at the other person to extract small talk (if their interests are seen through their physique, we must take advantage of them.) How?

You must become aware of empathy

Taking an interest in the mood of another person is the first step towards empathy. It is also an excellent way to start a conversation because it shortens the distances between the two interlocutors. This technique usually works primarily with the elderly, who are used to explaining things about their life. They do not present the same barriers, at a general level, as young people. They are much easier to access.

Give/receive a compliment

It is an excellent way to make Contact because it starts from some interest of the other interlocutor. To carry out this strategy, you have to learn to observe the people around us, and at this point, the knowledge you have of general social interests will also have an influence, which will help you detect them. The people who best receive compliments are usually the youngest since they are usually the ones who are most in touch with their interests and make them explicit about dressing, acting ...

Can you ask/give a favor?

When faced with a need, you can seek help from the people around you. It is one of the easiest ways to establish Contact and respect the distances that many people require. It is the best way to test the waters and see what a person's character is that a priori we have not just determined. Due to the distances it keeps, this technique helps immensely in adulthood since it encourages hierarchies (helped and helper).

Core Listening Skills

To respond appropriately to others, you need to pay attention to the messages they send and future associate responses with those messages. Active listening occurs when an individual manifests specific behavior that indicates that they are paying attention to the other person.

To better inform us of what they are telling us and show that we attend and are interested or not.

The listening signals regulate the conversation flow: we know when it is our turn when what we are telling is of interest, we allow them to continue talking ...

Components of active listening

Non-verbal components:

- Posture directed towards the interlocutor
- Attention facial expression
- Direct look

- Gestures and movements: affirmative movements with the head, smile

- Imitate ("mirror") the facial expression of the speaker

Verbal components (that signal to the speaker that they are paying attention and also encourage them to continue speaking):

- Murmurs of approval or denial: "Umm, Umm ...", "aha."

- Recognition responses: "Sure," "you're right," "I hear you," "I see ..."

- Explanatory summaries: "So ..."

- Ask a short question to clarify a point.

- Empathize: "I imagine how you feel," "I understand you" ...

- Reference to previous statements made by the other person (from remembering their name to remembering further details about facts, feelings, or ideas expressed by the other person) indicate an interest in them (when reflecting on what they have spoken on another occasion), and it is very likely that encourages her to participate more actively in the interaction that is taking place.

For good active listening, it is essential to:

- Do not carry out another activity while the other speaks.

- Wait for the other to finish. Avoid getting ahead of ourselves and guessing what the other wants to tell us.

- Concentrate on what the other is telling us—not thinking about what we will say to you later.

- Do not make value judgments: "That's nothing," "that's nonsense,"...

Conversation Mistakes

1. Avoid unpleasant gestures

Before verbal communication, there is body and gesture communication. If you are looking unfriendly, nervous, tense, or very angry or sad, it is impossible not to reflect on your body and face. It shows a lot.

Antidote: Take a deep breath before talking (especially if this is your first time talking to someone). Relax your body and imagine in your mind (that the conversation will be positive and productive). Look the other into the eyes, smile, and if you are not ready to talk, meet your friend at another time when you are more relaxed.

Motivation: "Breath, relax your body, smile, and let the words flow."

2. Constant complaints

Beware of turning conversations into an ocean of constant complaints and criticisms that tire, wear down, and consume a great deal of energy.

Antidote: If you want a pleasant conversation, let it flow with upbeat, fun, and motivating topics. If you need to solve a problem, choose another time to solve it and promptly.

Motivation: "Don't turn your conversations into battlefields. Life is too short to waste it on bad news."

3. Excessive prejudices

Having a series of limiting beliefs regarding the person in front of you affects the conversation. It shows in the content and body language.

Antidote: Question the beliefs that limit how you communicate with people who are not part of your environment, family, and friends. Changing your attitude is a progressive job that you can do at any time.

Practice the art of conversation when traveling. Read stories and biographies of people who have overcome significant obstacles in their life.

Take courses, training with different people. Participate in social and cooperative activities (they will help you generate understanding, accept the difference, and be more tolerant).

Motivation:

~ "Prejudices are the cause of misunderstandings, irrational fears, and you can lose a real friend."

~ "Mental barriers must be crossed to practice the art of conversing with the diversity of people that populate the planet."

4. Lack of attention and listening

Being in a thousand activities and constant stress influences you to lose your attention quickly, so you do not listen carefully to what the other person is telling you. When your mind is scattered, you can hardly dialogue with congruence and assertiveness.

The message you convey is: "I am not interested in the conversation, and the person who is with you notices it."

Antidote: for a bit of the rhythm of activities, especially if you want your conversations to be of quality and value. Practice active listening out of respect for yourself and the person who is with you.

How? Be present in the conversation, visually contracting, asking questions, sharing stories, experiences, smiling, and making the person feel comfortable and you too.

Motivation: "Mindfulness, listening, and the art of conversation can be worked on in-group communication and personal development workshops."

5. Talk to only criticize absent people

It is a mistake to criticize other people who are not present continually. Make a wrong impression on those who listen to you. The conversation becomes distorted, bitter, and feels emotions such as anger, sadness, and resentment.

Antidote: it is not worth spending time and energy talking about third parties and more if they are not present. Choose topics of conversation that positively nurture your friendship relationship and generate more pleasant emotions to raise your energy level.

Work with self-esteem and emotions if you feel that you cannot stop talking about third parties. And also try to solve conflicts directly with them.

Motivation: "Ask yourself: What am I aware of this attitude? How does it affect me, and how does it affect my relationship with others? What can I do to change my attitude? "

6. Talking excessively and always wanting to be right

Other relevant mistakes are always wanting to be right in the topics of conversation. Also, talking excessively and not letting the other person express. It is more common than we think.

It becomes dull, selfish, and shows a lack of empathy. This type of behavior does not favor the beginning of a friendship relationship. On the contrary, it causes estrangement and conflict.

Antidote: Check out why there is a need to focus the conversation only on you and your topics. An assertive discussion needs to be based on everyone's right to express themselves and active listening. You speak, I listen to you, and vice versa. Accompany by mutual positive reinforcement and understanding on an emotional level.

Motivation: "A conversation is richer and more fun when you both feel comfortable and understand each other. When problems arise, they are resolved in good spirits because the disposition of both is to solve and improve the relationship."

Being More Likable

1. Maintain eye contact

Maintaining eye contact is one of the minimum requirements for being pleasant in conversation, although it is not enough. You don't need to continually look into each other's eyes, as trying to do this is artificial and unsettling. It is best to look at the face of the person we are talking to and try not to push them away for long periods.

2. Take into account the cultural level of the other

Culture can be divided into many areas of knowledge. Assuming that they will understand the references you use or the concepts you use to explain something is not appropriate.

Think that if it is about technicalities or lines of reasoning belonging to very specialized areas of knowledge, and you use them regularly, you will make the other person uncomfortable. Not because they feel bad about not knowing what you're talking about, but because they have to interrupt to understand what you're saying.

3. Don't be afraid of silence

A good conversation can be full of silence. Therefore, it is better not to be afraid of those moments when no one speaks than to say anything to avoid having to go through those kinds of situations. What makes some silences uncomfortable is not the lack of words per se, but the context in which they occur and, above all, the way we react to them.

4. Show interest in the other person

The other person must be able to talk about what they consider important about the moment they are going through in a particular area of their life or their life in general, depending on the conversation's purpose. Ask questions about what might interest or concern him, and listen.

5. Don't adopt a patronizing attitude

Some people confuse the ability to advise on a subject that is mastered with the power to treat other people as if they were children or did not know anything about life. It is convenient to avoid this and consider that each person has their criteria and ability to understand what is best at all times.

6. Remember what matters about each person

The fact of remembering details about the people with whom we have spoken in the past shows interest, and in general, it is responded with gratitude by others, especially if what we keep in our memory is something personal beyond the necessary data such as name or age.

7. Use relaxed non-verbal language

Try not to use non-verbal language that shows you are defensive. For example, keeping your arms crossed or slouching where you are sitting as you speak. It is better to be relaxed, with the limbs relatively far from the vertical that marks our thorax.

8. Take care of your hygiene

Beyond the style you use to dress, hygiene is essential. The simple fact of not respecting this guideline makes people physically more distant, with the consequent impact on social relationships.

Being More Fun

Prepare yourself a little

Jotting down one to three topics before the conversation started reduces anxiety during the conversation and increases the interaction's enjoyment. "Even just thinking of an idea or two in the twenty seconds leading up to the small talk seems to help.

Start the conversation on the right foot

That gives people a topic or trivia to keep the conversation going.

Fine also starts conversations by saying things like:

- What do you do for fun?
- What is your favorite outfit to wear in quarantine?
- Tell me about the best you have eaten so far

Avoid trying to outdo the other person

Yes, the situation is difficult for both of you, and you might feel that you are showing compassion - I understand you! Life is hard for me too! - but that makes the other person feel underappreciated. So, don't do the following:

- First friend: "Ash, I've had Zoom meetings all day. I am completely exhausted."
- Second friend: "Do you think that's bad? At the end of my workday, I have to entertain and feed two teenagers."
- First friend: "I feel claustrophobic now that the parks and trails are closed."

- Second friend: "Try living in a one-bedroom apartment in Brooklyn."

Assertiveness Skills

Assertiveness is a social skill that allows us to express our rights, opinions, ideas, needs, and feelings in a conscious, straightforward, honest, and sincere way without hurting or harming others. When we communicate assertively, we act from an inner state of self-confidence and self-affirmation instead of limiting emotions such as anxiety, guilt, rage, or anger.

The components of assertiveness

- Take the situation and context into account
- Trust that your ideas are valid and deserve to be expressed
- Manage your feelings and put them into words
- Aware of what you feel in the midst of what is likely to be a difficult and intense situation
- Understand the other people involved, imagining how they feel and why

By putting these five skills together, you will be able to say what you need to say appropriately to the context, situation, and people involved so that the message recipients can process it without raising their defenses. This point is significant. Remember that talking to an individual who is on the defensive is like talking to the wall. Your message will not reach him.

Four ways to develop assertiveness

As you can see, assertiveness is a skill set, and that is why it can be difficult for you. However, it is possible to learn to be assertive and to improve your skills. Some ways you can do it are as follows:

- Pay more attention to your feelings, all the time.

- Befriend your emotions. When you value your feelings, they become a powerful tool. They will let you know when you need to defend yourself or speak. They will give you motivation and energy when you need them most.

- Start building your emotional management skills, for example, by increasing your vocabulary and using it daily.

- Take every opportunity that comes your way to defend yourself to the best of your ability. If you missed an opportunity, reflect on what you should have done.

- Practice makes perfect. The more you do it, the easier it will be to be assertive.

Chapter 13. Forming and Growing Friendships

"Friendship is a soul that lives in two bodies; a heart that dwells in two souls.". - Aristotle

Introduction to the Process of Making Friends

For the vast majority of people making new friends is an otherworldly skill.

Still, let me tell you, you are in the right place. Because your social skills can be cultivated, if you manage to have many friends and influence them, your life will be better and get many rewards.

You have heard it well: "Who has a friend, has a treasure."

Even if you are a person who feels lonely, the truth is more in-depth than you think.

While it is true that there are people with the skill to attract friends, they were not born with those skills. These people with hundreds of friends learned it in their early childhood, and they have it tattooed in their subconscious. So, I hope you are not lost. You can do it too: make friends and feel supported.

But in another sense, having good friends is difficult. Otherwise, there would not be so many services and web pages to find people to interact with.

Why does it cost so much?

In the first place, many people believe that friendship should be "born" naturally and that the opposite is not authentic.

But the main reason is the lack of continuity. As easy as this. Constant Contact is one of the pillars to create a friendship. Do you remember when you were little? You used to see your classmates almost every day, but now that you have a job or family, that is practically impossible.

That is why your workplace can be one of the best places to make friends if you can create bonds beyond the professional relationship. If not, building new friendships becomes difficult as you get older.

There are a series of strategies to make someone you just met like:

~ Create a time limit at the beginning, so you know that you won't be stuck talking to you and feel more comfortable

~ Show real interest by facing your whole body towards him

~ Say their name often and make sure they get to know yours as soon as possible

~ Asking him for a small favor (the so-called Ben Franklin effect for the way the Pennsylvania governor earned the appreciation of his political rivals)

These little techniques are beneficial to like more, but they are not usually enough to create a real friendship relationship. Below, let's see how you can find potential friends.

Finding Potential Friends

If you are looking to make new friends, you must be clear about what kind of friends you want to make. If you need soul friends (best friends like brothers), keep reading! Those friends are people with whom you can talk about everything. You may or may not meet every day, but it doesn't matter since the strength of your friendship is not determined by how often you meet. It is more than that. These are the friends you can count on when you need them, and they will go the extra mile for you.

How to find them?

1. Realize that your fear is in your head

The first step is to develop a healthy mental image about meeting new people. Some of us see meeting new people as a scary event. We are concerned about making a good impression, whether the other person will like you, how to keep the conversation going. The more you think about it, the scarier it seems. This initial apprehension turns into a mental fear, which takes on a life of its own and unknowingly prevents you from making new friends. Shyness towards others is the result of fear.

In reality, all these fears are in your head. If you think about it,

99% of people are too busy worrying about these very things to pay attention to the details. While they are concerned about the impression made, they are worried about the image they will make. They are just as scared as you are. The remaining 1% are people who recognize that a relationship is based on much stronger values than words or specific things to say/do during a single encounter. Even if people judge you based on what you do/say, are these people you want to be friends with? I do not think so.

2. Start small with the people you know

If you haven't been socializing a lot, meeting a bunch of new people can seem intimidating. If so, start small first. Reduce the task's difficulty by starting with your inner circle of friends, people with whom you are most familiar. Some ways to do that:

- Contact your acquaintances

Do you have 'hello' friends from previous years? Or friends you lost touch with overtime? Leave a friendly SMS and say hello. Ask for a meeting when they're free. See if there are opportunities to reconnect.

- See if there are circles you can join

Circles are established groups of friends. The idea is not to enter any group but to introduce yourself through an acquaintance. With friend circles, existing members will likely take the lead in conversations, so you can only take an observer's role and observe the dynamics between other people.

- Meet the friends of your friends

You can join them on their outings or just ask your friend to introduce them to you. If you're comfortable with your friends, there's a good chance that he's pleased with them too.

Making Plans with Potential Friends

- Accept invitations to go out

I have friends who rarely go out. When they are asked out, they decline most invitations because they prefer to stay home. As a result, their social circles are limited. If you want to have more friends, you need to get out of your comfort zone and go out more often. You can't make more friends in real life if you stay at home!

3. Get out on the street

Once you become more familiar with your inner circle of friends, the next step will be to reach out to people you don't know.

Join gathering groups: Meetup.com is an excellent social networking site. There are many interest groups such as groups for entrepreneurs, aspiring authors, vegans, lovers of board games, cycling enthusiasts. Choose your interests and join those groups. Meetings are usually monthly, depending on the group itself—a great way to quickly meet lots of new people.

Attend workshops/courses: These serve as central avenues that bring like-minded people together. I went to a salsa workshop and met many great people, some of whom I became very close friends.

Voluntary: Great way to kill 2 birds with one stone - not only do you get to spread kindness and contribution, but you also meet compassionate people with a cause.

Party: Parties such as birthday parties, Christmas/New Year parties/celebrations, housewarming, functions/events. It's probably a place where you'll make many new friends, but not necessarily quality relationships. But it is an excellent way to meet more people.

Visit bars and clubs: Many people go to meet more friends, but I don't recommend them, as the friends you make here are probably more hello-bye friends rather than type 2 or 3 friends. Good to go a couple of times and see how it turns out first to pass judgment.

Online communities: The Internet is a great way to meet new people. The blogs of your interest are a start. Some of my best friends started online. Participate constructively and add value to the discussion. You will soon get to know the people there better

4. Take the first step

Once you are with people around you, someone has to take the first step. If the other party doesn't start a conversation, take the first step to say hello. Get to know each other a little better! Share something about yourself and then give the other party a chance to share about him/her. Like asking what the day is like or what they did today/last week, something comfortable is a good conversation starter. Once the ice is broken, it will be easier to connect.

5. Be open

- Be open-minded. Do not judge

Sometimes you can have a predetermined notion of the type of friend you want. Maybe someone you understand listens, has the same hobbies, watches the same movies, has similar educational levels. When you meet the person, you realize that they differ from your expectations and you are disappointed.

Do not do that. Give friendship a chance to flourish. More importantly, give yourself a chance with this friendship. I have several excellent friends who come from totally different backgrounds, and I would never have thought that we would be this close when I met them, simply because we are so different.

- Open your heart

On the same note, open your heart to the person. This connection between you and the other party can only begin when your heart is open. It means trusting, having faith, and believing in the goodness of others. You cannot establish a new connection if you distrust others or are afraid that things will not work out. You'll send out the wrong vibes and make them close their hearts to you too.

6. Meet the person

Friendship is about you and the other person. Get to know the person as an individual. Here are some questions to consider:

- What does he or she do?

- Which are your hobbies?

- What have you been doing recently?
- What are your next priorities/goals?
- What do you value the most?
- What are your values?
- What motivates/drives you?
- What are your passions in life? Goals? Dreams?

7. Connect without expecting anything in return

Often, we are too caught up with our concerns, like what others will think of us, what we should say next, our next action, that we miss the whole point of friendship. You can work on aspects of the presentation, like how you look, what you say, and how you say things, but don't get hung up on it. These actions do not (truly) define friendship. What determines the company is the connection between you and the friend.

Show warmth, love, and respect for everyone you meet. Do things because you want to and not because you have to. Take care of them as you would yourself. By approaching others authentically, you will attract people who genuinely want to connect. Among them will be your future real friends.

8. Be yourself

Don't change to make new friends. That is the worst thing you can do. Why do I say that?

Let's say you make a lot of new friends by being daring and up for anything. However, your usual self is calm and introverted. What happens then? Initially, it can be great to have these new friends, but the friendship was established with you being an extrovert. That means:

- Be still the daring and upbeat person your new friends met you with. But it will only be a facade. In the long run, it will be exhausting to maintain this image. Not only that, the friendship will be built on an open front. OR

- Switch back to the introvert. Now your friends will feel cheated because this is not the person they became friends with. They will also gradually drift away if their personalities don't match.

So, just be yourself. That way, potential new friends will get to know you as you do and use it to decide if they want to take the friendship one step further. I don't think you need to be outgoing and articulate like Tony Robbins to make friends. It's about being you. The most faithful friendships are built with both parties accepting each other for who they are.

9. Be there for them

A friendship is a supportive union between two people. Do any of your friends currently need help? Is there something you can help them with? How can you better support them?

When you help your friends, don't do it with the expectation of being allowed next time. Instead, it helps unconditionally. Treat them with emotional generosity. Give because you want to, not because you feel compelled to.

10. Make an effort to stay in touch

It takes an ongoing effort to maintain a friendship. The willingness to make an effort is what differentiates great friends from acquaintances. Invite your friends out once in a while. Depending on the friendship's intensity, there is no need to meet every few days or once a week; catching up once a month or once every few months might be enough.

The strength of your relationship is not measured by how often you meet. For some of my best friends, we meet only once every few months. But there is never any doubt that we are closely connected and will be there for each other when needed.

If you both have your own set of commitments, it can be challenging to find time together. Host a simple gathering, say over lunch, coffee, or dinner. Or they can always catch up on text messages, WhatsApp, or phone calls. Technology has made communication so easy that it's hard not to stay in touch.

Deepening New Friendships

It would be absurd for me to give you a list of questions or answers so that you could memorize them and let them go without rhyme or reason in your conversations. That would be like giving you a paintbrush without you knowing how to paint.

Therefore, although some steps may surprise you, what you will learn next is how to use the psychological mechanisms that allow us to connect with others to your advantage.

How to deepen new friendships?

1. Make it a priority

Think wisely. How often do you meet your friends? Do you only meet for specific reasons like celebrating a birthday or going out for drinks?

In those situations, it is difficult for deep conversations to arise. Therefore, you must look for the opportunity for it.

And you must make it a priority. If your excuse for not doing it is that you don't have time, find another one. There is never a lack of time. There is only a lack of interest.

Tip #1: Every two weeks, write or call one of your friends for no apparent reason, just to meet up and catch up. You will be building the foundations of a much deeper relationship.

2. Show them your support

Something that friends often do is pick each other up. Yes, they are little jokes (some very funny), but when the only thing that is recognized is negative, we make it difficult for people to want to open up with us.

Why do you do it then?

The culprit is the Schadenfreude effect. Remembering in front of your friends how ridiculous one of them is made when his/her pants ripped at his/her wedding makes you feel momentarily better.

The closer and similar to you someone seems to you, the more you are comforted by their misfortunes. It is cruel, but it is part of human nature. Compare yourself with others and believe that their failures benefit you in some way.

A simple compliment to a friend can be as powerful as giving them cash, and it has even been shown that by rejoicing in their achievements, we can make them feel more understood and appreciated.

It strengthens the relationship and prepares it for more in-depth exchanges of ideas.

It is also essential that you support their image of themselves and make them feel good about their achievements. It is necessary to turn a friend into a best friend with whom you can share everything.

Tip #2: Don't just exploit your friends' funny moments. Show them that they have qualities that you admire and get them to relive their good times with you.

3. Get interested and stop being interesting

Before you start delving into specific topics, you must make sure that you have created a minimal connection, or all your attempts will fail.

To achieve this, the first thing is to be interested in your interlocutor because the best way to improve a relationship is simply by listening.

To master the art of caring for others, stop thinking of conversations as tennis games. You don't have to return the ball.

It is better to imagine that you are a detective with the objective is to find something surprising in your interlocutor.

And do you know the best of all? That when you start to care for others, they will also want to know more about you.

The habit of really listening without waiting for your turn to speak is rare. But the people who do it can connect with whomever they want.

Tip #3: Don't try to impress in your conversations. If you want to create a greater connection, you just have to be interested in them.

4. Find emotional ties

The next key to connecting is finding a link.

Although the idea is that you share more points in common, the better, there are some more powerful than others: emotional ties.

If you are interested in your interlocutor during the conversation, there will come a time when one of your questions will click and connect with one of his/her passions. Then you will see that he begins to speak with tremendous enthusiasm and intensity.

When it's done, you can try linking to this topic. If, for example, the other person was talking about his/her passion for skydiving and you like it too, you already have a common interest. Your conversation will begin to flow without difficulty.

But what if you are terrified of skydiving? Can't link anymore?

If that were so, there would only be a small fraction of humanity you could connect with. In these cases, don't bond out of interest but out of emotion.

Look a little further than what he is telling you. Okay, he likes skydiving. But why? What makes you feel? What values are hidden behind?

Maybe it makes him feel alive, and you can bond with that emotion through another activity that makes you feel alive too. For that, you could comment that you feel the same going to a rock concert, for example.

Try not to stay only in their opinions and comments because the logic behind them is emotions.

For example, some studies have shown that one of the themes capable of creating the most incredible connection is travel because we all identify with the values and emotions behind traveling: freedom, experiencing the new, and learning.

Once you have established an emotional bond, you can move on to the next point.

Tip #4: Find common ground with your interlocutor to strengthen your connection. Ideally, you share the same emotions and values.

5. Use vulnerability

Although it will cost you at first, this may be the behavior that will help you the most to deepen your relationships.

It is about revealing some personal information that makes you vulnerable.

Often the strongest bond between two people is the trust created after one or both have shared something about their fears, shortcomings, or insecurities.

For many, this is nonsense. Many believe that by showing weaknesses, people will take advantage of them or reject them. And so, they are not able to connect.

But if you look closely, you have probably created the most potent ties with people who know some personal aspects of your life. Giving them that space will help them see you as someone more human and with whom they can connect.

You don't have to start by uncovering your most intimate secret. Start with something a little more personal than you would generally say, for example, by discussing a problem at work, and see how the other responds. You will usually restore the trust by empathizing with you and revealing something personal about you.

Tip #5: If you want to connect more deeply with someone, allow them to get to know your real self, even if it means stepping out of your comfort zone a bit.

6. Raise the level of conversation

Most conversations have a natural progression as if it were a relationship. But sometimes, some get stuck in trivia.

What can you do in this case?

There is a hierarchy of vulnerability in our interactions that will allow you to create connections to address more significant emotional significance issues.

The progression is as follows:

Phatic phase: they are expressions without emotional content: "How are you?"

Fact-based phase: you share information (perhaps personal), but there are no emotions or opinions linked: "Yesterday I finished my studies."

Evaluation phase: here, you express opinions, but not beliefs: "The graduation was very exciting."

Emotional phase: things are starting to get interesting. While the types above of communication are based on judgment, this one is based on emotions. It is where you show your vulnerability: "I was sad that you didn't come."

Peak phase: the most emotionally vulnerable level. You share deep feelings that reveal so much about you, so you can't be sure how others will respond. "I think deep down I'm terrified of losing you."

Tip #5: Use emotional communication at its best. Talk about your feelings to connect with others.

7. Ask for their opinion and advice

So far, you have seen how to connect with people, the importance of showing your vulnerabilities, and the best way to communicate to deepen your relationships.

But how do you bring out a topic you want to talk about?

Too easy. Ask for advice.

Asking advice is a remarkably effective way to get people involved in an issue and want to know their point of view. By asking for their point of view, you get them to put themselves in your shoes and see the world from their eyes.

Tip #7: When you want to delve into a topic in a conversation, ask for your interlocutor's opinion. The more connection you have with him, the more enriching the discussion can be.

Making a Group of Friends

1.Introduce yourself to the group

Join clubs, teams, and activities to meet your future friends. Be aware of what group members do in their spare time and do those activities if they interest you. They will soon have experiences to share, which will serve as a natural basis for forming a friendship.

2.Spend time alone with each member of the group

If you try to force yourself into a large group with immediate exits, it will be overwhelming. Develop strong friendships with each person first and use these friendships as bridges to reach the rest of the group.

3.Suggest activities to a group member and ask him or her to invite the rest of the group

You don't have to wait for any invitations. You can create your opportunities by organizing social outings.

- The activity you plan does not have to be elaborate. It can be a simple outing to the mall, a movie night, or a basketball game. If your family has a pool or lives near a fun destination, invite people to your house.

- Make sure you are comfortable doing whatever activity you propose so that you feel relieved.

4. Tell your friends that you want to hang out with the group

If you feel very comfortable with a friend's company, just be honest and express your desire to meet others.

It's essential to have a casual tone so you don't sound too eager. Just say something like, "Your friends look funny. It would be great to get to know them better.

5. Build confidence before going out with the group for the first time

When you have confidence in yourself, you radiate positive energy that attracts others. Work on your confidence, sit down with a sheet of paper, and write down your positive qualities.

6. Use confident body language to make a good impression

Practice good posture to look self-confident. Smile to show the group that you are friendly and calm. You should also make eye contact to establish a connection with others while showing confidence in yourself.

Looking Forward as Your Social Skills Improve

Social skills are those behaviors that allow you to relate to others. It is essential to work on your actions and reactions.

How to improve your Social Skills?

1. Learn the "broken record" technique

Even if it has a strange and funny name, it can be beneficial to us. It is about the constant repetition of an idea that we would like to express. You can also say a phrase several times.

For example, the employees of a telephone exchange: No matter what the customer tells them, they always respond in the same way, as if they were a machine.

2. Understand social fears

Are you shy or anxious in a meeting or conversation (especially with people you don't know)? It is essential to identify your degree of introversion and what emotions you experience in those situations. You may want to do specific techniques, so you don't feel that way.

3. Think before reacting to criticism

Nobody likes to be evaluated, criticized, or examined, especially if the results are not expected. When someone tells us their opinion to help us, it is essential to receive that comment as a compliment and not negatively.

So the next time they give you an answer that you don't like, stop for a moment and analyze why they told you that. Instead of getting angry, react without giving too much justification.

4. Take an interest in others

Everyone loves to talk about themselves and those around them. There is nothing better than asking questions and listening to the other to gain someone's trust and improve your social skills.

Show interest in what he is saying, and in this way, you will become his friend or, at least, a good companion. Being interested in the other makes you attractive.

5. Use the sandwich technique

Just as you don't like to receive criticism, neither do others. Therefore, if you have to say something negative about the other person, it is better to use this technique more than adequate.

~ It begins with a positive aspect, continues with the one that could be improved (criticism), and finally ends with phrases of confidence and encouragement.

For example: "You have notably improved your performance. However, you still need to increase your production. You can do it! "

6. Use empathy

One of the foundations of social skills is understanding what you feel and what motivates whomever you have in front of you. Remember the phrase "treat others as you would like to be treated," but keep in mind what others want.

Being more empathetic offers many advantages. For example, it is being liked by people better, being persuasive, understanding what's going on around you.

To improve your empathy, we recommend paying attention to the interlocutor's words and gestures: glances, silences, hand movements. Try to imagine what motivates him and why he acts in such a way and make him feel heard and understood.

7. Repeat what the other feels

It is not about speaking like a parrot or like an echo. But about showing that we have understood the message. Do your best not to sound forced or superficial.

For example:

~ I know this promotion is essential to you…

~ I know your concerns regarding…

~ I understand your fears….

8. Be assertive

Proper communication doesn't just improve your social skills. Also, it allows you to express your needs, express your opinions, and make honest suggestions.

Many times, we passively accept certain situations to avoid conflicts. That difficulty in saying "no" can work against us.

To be more assertive, you must replace your negative thoughts. Understand that others cannot read minds and remember your goals or priorities.

Also, we recommend that you be specific when expressing your reasons. Don't feel selfish or the wrong person for not being available to the other.

9. Show affection

Who doesn't like to receive signs of affection? Although sometimes our reaction is embarrassment or shyness, the truth is that we all love to feel loved.

Receiving and giving affection is very important to improve our social skills and have healthy relationships. A hug, a caress, a smile, or a word of encouragement can be very useful. Don't forget to offer compliments and compliments as long as they are genuine.

10. Convinces naturally

Persuasion is an art that must be worked on continuously. There are several techniques to achieve it. For example, they are doing a favor to the other so that they feel obliged on a moral level and return it to us somehow. Although this may be questionable ethics, it is up to you where to set the limits.

In any case, you may not be able to improve your social skills on your own. If this is your case, we recommend that you consult a psychologist who can help you with it.

Chapter 14. Conversation

Have you ever wondered what would happen if we couldn't talk? How would you communicate with your friends, with your family, or with your colleagues? The conversation is essential, and we occupy it daily and at all times. Next, you will know its definition and main characteristics.

The conversation is when two or more people talk about a specific topic. For example, "Favorite Food," as the following conversation shows:

> Peter: I want to know what your favorite food is, can you tell me?
> Sean: I love French fries.
> Peter: Just the fries?
> Camila: No, I love them with chicken.
> Sean: Yes! I love chicken too.

In this conversation, they change the exchange information. That is, now Peter already knows which is Sean and Camila's favorite food. That is, he has new information that allows him to know them better.

Thus, the purpose of any conversation is to exchange information between the people who participate, which allows them to get to know each other better.

The conversation has the following characteristics:

- It is spontaneous; that is, it develops naturally and is not prepared
- The conversation is characterized by being familiar and expressive
- You can use gestures, mimics, movements to converse
- The volume, rhythm, and tone of voice, likewise, provide information in a conversation
- The theme is defined by those who participate in this activity. Thus, a conversation about music can end in another topic that has nothing to do with it

With conversation, you can inform, communicate, express joys or sorrows, advise, recommend, relate, argue, present ideas, etc.

Just as a conversation has its characteristics, it also has The Secret Flow. In the section below, I will show you. Keep reading!

The Secret of Conversation Flow

What is the secret flow of the conversation?

Flow is the operational state of mind in which a person is completely immersed in the activity that he/she performs. It is characterized by focusing on energy, total involvement with the task, and success in acting. This sensation is experienced while the activity is in progress.

So, conversation is a daily activity of all people. And just as it is essential in personal relationships, it is also necessary for organizations.

In the work environment, a person interacts with colleagues, superiors, clients, etc. Similarly, he/she receives information, gives or receives instructions, and coordinates with work teams. All these tasks and relationships involve conversation, hence the importance of achieving the flow of conversation.

The flow of the conversation allows any interlocutor to understand the entire communication. This conversation gives you both indications to see the interest of the other in what it is saying. Both of you have a clear understand and know if you want to intervene or if you want to interrupt.

1. Don't do a thousand things at once

It is manual. We have conversations while we think about what the boss has told us or what we will do after work, and we even talk while answering a WhatsApp from work. Focus on the conversation and make the other person feel that you are there. If you want to get out of the talk, do not make the other person feel boring.

2. Don't be uncompromising

You need to start any conversation, assuming you have something new to learn. Do not minimize the other person comparing him/her with you, your studies, and any other thing.

Don't use conversations as a constant promotion. It usually happens. A new one comes to work and spends a few months answering each question from his/her colleagues, especially bosses as if the job interview had not ended. Or they sell you their blogs in vein. Relax and enjoy more.

3. Help yourself with journalism

To make the conversation useful, think about the who, what, how, when, and why. If you ask someone something complicated, you will get a simple answer. Don't think for them; let them explain themselves and ask something more straightforward like: 'what did you feel?' instead of were you terrified? '

4. Respect the pace of the conversation

It often happens to us that when we come up with something brilliant, we hold it in our heads and wait for the other to finish speaking it before releasing it and receiving the imaginary ovation from the audience. The problem is that sometimes what you think is not so brilliant, and you tend to lose the thread of the conversation and to make matters worse ... Sometimes you forget before saying it.

5. If you don't know what it is ... Say it

Nothing happens because you do not know the latest gossip in the neighborhood or that you do not remember who invented penicillin. If you don't know, better say so, or you'll be.

6. Don't repeat yourself.

We all do it, and many times we do not realize it. But change it; it is real torture for those around you ... We have all seen that guy repeating the same thing over and over again in a debate.

7. Listen.

Alpha Male Bible | 287

Buddha said, "If your mouth is open, you are not learning. If you are not listening to the other person and analyzing what he is saying, you are simply not in the conversation."

8. Be brief.

We all know that person who can't stop talking. We know what we all think of her and what is said when she leaves. Don't be that person.

And he concludes: "Go out. Talk to people and listen to them. And most importantly: prepare to be surprised."

Invitation: The Art of Good Questions

Questions can be asked in different ways. The four most common types of questions are:

- indirect
- open
- mirror
- closed

Indirect questions

In some circumstances, mainly in negotiation situations, when needs detection is beginning, it may be more convenient to invite to speak or request information than to ask questions.

Ultimately it is about asking, but indirectly. This form is less aggressive and helps create a cooperative environment.

Invites to express the needs of the other negotiating party, avoiding stress. Some examples:

> I would like to know your point of view on ...
> I'm sure you have an opinion on ...
> I would appreciate it if you could honestly explain what you think about ...
> I don't know if you agree with me that ...

Open questions

They have two purposes:

> Encourage the interlocutor to keep talking: "And what happened then?" "What do you do afterward?" "How did the contract end?"
> Delve into some questions on which you want more information: "How do you usually send your orders?" "What criteria do your clients use to identify the quality of the service?" "When do you think we can re-negotiate the pending fringes?"

They usually begin with the words "how", "why", "where", "who", "when", "what", "in what way ,,,".

Mirror questions

Its objective is to encourage the interlocutor to deepen or expand an issue.

For example, when the interlocutor explains: "In our company, we manage production through a synchronized system," ask: "A synchronized system?"

A mirror question has the function of requesting more

information ("What do you understand by the synchronized system?"), But it provides greater agility to the communication process.

However, you must not abuse this type of question to give the impression that you repeat or copy (as if it were an echo) what the other person says.

Closed questions

The answer you are looking for can be "yes" or "no" or some specific quantity, word, or phrase. They can have various purposes:

- Choose between two alternatives: Will they pay it in cash or by bank check?
- Persuade: Don't you think this is the right solution for both parties?
- Specify or clarify a question: When you speak of deferred payment, what period are you referring to?
- Request a decision: Shall we sign the agreement next week?
- Close a topic: Do you agree with this approach?

And additionally, a piece of advice: Be careful with "why?" Questions.

At some point in the negotiation process, it may happen that the reason or motive behind the positions, statements, proposals, or rejections of your interlocutor is not apparent.

Often, a question formulated in this way gives the interlocutor the impression that he has to justify or defend his point of view. As a reaction, a negative attitude of position defense can be obtained.

Bonus: Ten Easy Tips for Improving Conversation

Learn your message. What is left to improvisation does not usually turn out, and what is rehearsed and developed previously. Whether you have a one-on-one conversation or are speaking to an audience: rehearse.

2. Make the other person feel important. Human beings seek to be recognized and taken into account. Something as simple as repeating your interlocutor's name from time to time or showing sincere interest is one way to achieve this.

3. Use accessible and forward-thinking language. Your way of speaking has to be elegant, kind, and cheerful. Nobody is influenced by negative people who complain more than necessary or who mistreat words and language.

4. Relax and breathe. Whenever you communicate, everything will turn out much better if you relax, and your nervousness will not spread to others.

5. Focus on finding joint solutions that satisfy the parties in one way or another. Always think of the whole, that all parties can feel that they gain something.

6. Take care of your non-verbal language. Do not hold on to both hands or cross them. Stay in an open position; show your palms from time to time. Express with gestures.

7. Make a slow argument when the going gets tough. Some

tension can appear in any conversation. If you detect those moments and take the opportunity to take more breaks, you will do better.

8. Make the most of the silence. It is understood as a reflective pause. The one who maintains the silence causes the other person to think, maintains the balance of power of the conversation, and increases their security.

9. Do not criticize or put yourself against anyone. Even if you disagree with something, do not attack or speak ill of others, and especially if things are not going well, do not turn against your interlocutor. Use expressions such as "I understand what you are saying. However, it would be positive to consider ... "or" I agree with you on .... although perhaps we should talk about… »are expressions that serve to reach agreements.

10. Never lose control. In communication, the one who loses control and uses inappropriate forms loses the game and undoubtedly the tournament. Our brain remembers for many years those outbursts of some people around us. For this reason, maintaining an emotional state is always; I always repeat, necessary, and healthy for your communication.

Conclusion

Meeting other people is a typical activity of our ordinary life. Walking through the streets, entering the bus, standing on the ramp waiting for the train to arrive when boarding the plane, climbing a ladder, at work, college, at home, at the doctor's office, the movies, the beach, and so on. In the least expected place, you can start an enjoyable small talk. When we feel comfortable talking to a person, we want to speak to them again soon. The opposite occurs when the person, apart from being uninformed, has an attitude, a short and poor vocabulary, which makes them incapable of having a friendly conversation. That is why no one wants to talk to someone negative again.

We have seen a lot about small talk, like when with whom to do small talk. In this book, too, we have taught that you can convey your feelings, emotions, intellectual, social, cultural level, and principles through small talk. The other person can do the same. So, there are many topics that you can treat. They are, for example, family, entertainment, studies, travel, food, places visited. There is no need to interfere in the other's personal life, violate their privacy, and much less deal with specific delicate issues such as skin color, overweight people, preferences, sexuality, race, religion, or making judgments about elements of cultures.

You can have an excellent small talk about unimportant topics, awards, weather, sports, cars, houses, trips, a book that has just been read, etc. because what you want is to maintain a light and simple conversation where the skills and similarities, not each be contrary to what is said.

Often, in communication, some limit themselves to misunderstanding, to take for granted concepts and ideas that do not conform to what the interlocutor informs them. Knowing how to dialogue, argue, and listen is key to saving us meaningless conflicts.

As I have put it in the book, it is clear that anyone can feel afraid to start a conversation. But you don't have to feel that way as we have put together a set of steps, tips, strategies, and tricks to help you overcome that fear.

To conclude, there is a saying: "by the mouth, the fish dies." That has everything to do with what we talk about. The important thing is to speak little and reasonable and prepare to address any conversation topic with anyone, whenever and wherever.